D1247202

PEACHTREE STREET, USA

Celestine Sibley

Photos by JOHN BAZEMORE

Peachtree Publishers, Ltd.

Published by
PEACHTREE PUBLISHERS, LTD.
494 Armour Circle, N.E.
Atlanta, Georgia 30324

Manufactured in the United States of America

Library of Congress Catalog Card Number 86-61546

ISBN 0-934601-04-6

Design by Paulette L. Lambert

1st printing

Contents

Preface

This book was originally published by Doubleday & Company in 1963, the second book I had written and one which I dearly loved. When Peachtree Publishers acquired the right to reissue it in 1986, I was jubilant because it had been out of print and therefore as good as dead for a number of years. But that was no reason to turn naive and fatuous when editor Chuck Perry asked me to update it. I know as well as anyone that in twenty-three years everything in Atlanta has changed three or four times, but when Chuck said, "How about updating it?" I said happily, "Oh, sure!"

"Didn't you know," a friend of mine inquired somberly, "that the only fixed and immutable fact about Atlanta is that the Yankees won the war?"

That's not quite true. The fact of change, growth, continuing surprises and excitement prevails. Atlanta is not a boring, stodgy, set-in-its-ways city. That you can count on. And besides, who can be sure the Yankees really did win that war? Victorious in battle, perhaps, but won over and assimilated in peace.

There have been sad changes and great changes. Some wonderful people have died or moved away — wise, funny, colorful people it was a joy to write about. New, outrageous and totally captivating people have moved in. In 1963 most of us hadn't heard of Ted Turner, for instance, and the other day some far traveler told me that there are foreigners who know our town only as the home of that movie star-handsome entrepreneur who may one day own us all. He already brags that he's billions of dollars in debt with a personal fortune estimated at a mere $500 million.

Turner was born in Cincinnati and moved to Georgia when he was nine years old. In 1963 at the age of twenty-four years, he was busy turning his father's billboard business into the biggest outdoor advertising company in the South.

He first attracted attention by his expertise as a sailor, winning the America's Cup in 1977. He had bought a low-power UHF television station in Atlanta which metamorphosed into the Super-Station, beaming signals 22,300 miles into space, bouncing them off a satellite and taking news twenty-four hours a day into more than thirty-three million homes. He owns the city's baseball team, the Braves, and its basketball team, the Hawks; he owns eighty percent of MGM-United Artists, the movie company; he tried to buy CBS; and he started his own Olympics with the Goodwill Games in Moscow in the summer of 1986.

Turner is one of the new breed of colorful Atlanta achievers, a sassy fellow with a seaman's philosophy — "When you're in rough seas, keep moving."

Then there's John Portman, the architect-builder who is author of some of Atlanta's more astounding buildings, most spectacularly the seventy-three-story Peachtree Plaza hotel, a dark-mirrored silo which stands tall and unmatched on the skyline.

Due to Portman and many other Atlanta builders, old-timers looking at our town from a skyscraper window or that favorite viewing spot, the Jackson Street hill, where Margaret Mitchell once lived, are baffled by towering buildings they can't identify. Time was when you could call their names with the affection and familiarity of a hunter calling his hounds.

"They build so *fast*," a man complained the other day. "Turn your back and there's another one!"

The latest thing on nearby Copenhill, from which Gen. William

T. Sherman directed the Battle of Atlanta, is a series of pancake-shaped circular buildings housing the new Jimmy Carter Presidential Library and a part of Emory University's vast archives. This despite a prolonged citizen's squabble against having a highway, called a parkway, built to the library. The library opened in the fall of 1986. The parkway project is still in the hands of the courts.

Perhaps the most far-reaching physical change to come to our town in these last two decades is the Metropolitan Atlanta Rapid Transit Authority system, familiarly called MARTA by its passengers. The system, still far from finished, sprouts rails and bus lines out in all directions, giving citizens from several counties easy and relatively cheap transportation. A woman I know has been taking advantage of so-called Senior Citizen airplane flights all over the country since she found out that she can get to the airport by MARTA for sixty cents.

"I know it's silly," she said, "but I used to feel so frustrated when I had to spend so much just to get started."

On a purely personal note, I moved outside Atlanta — to a log cabin in what was pure country twenty-five miles away just before this book was published the first time. The cabin was old (1840) and had to be propped up and rebuilt, but before we had actually moved in I used to take my typewriter and sit in the quiet of its dilapidated walls to work on the final chapters of *Peachtree Street, U.S.A.* My daughter and son-in-law, newly out of the Army, came to Atlanta to job and house hunt and brought their baby to stay with me while they looked. I worked with John sleeping — or howling — on a pillow in a box at my feet. That baby, now twenty-three years old, is a photographer for *The Clayton News/Daily* and is responsible for the pictures in this book.

And this is perhaps the place to mention two other people who helped me cope with the accumulated changes the years brought — Betty Parham, a tireless researcher, and Lillian King, who is unintimidated by computers.

Atlanta City Hall, as seen from the Capitol grounds

Why Do We Love It?

CHAPTER I

A few years ago the police picked up an elderly and eccentric Atlanta citizen on complaint of her neighbors that she was throwing rocks at and using what the law fastidiously referred to as "opprobrious words" to passing children.

It was a hot August day and the old lady wore not only a wool dress but a heavy winter coat to cover it. When the police matron made her undress for the routine delousing shower, it was discovered that she also wore, tied here and there about her person in little cloth bags, $10,500 in cash.

"Loony," said the officers who happened to know that she had been subsisting for years out of Broad Street garbage cans.

"Yeah," agreed the police matron sympathetically. "She doesn't belong here. She belongs in Milledgeville State Hospital."

"Milledgeville . . . don't be absurd!" put in the old lady crisply. "I'm not *that* crazy and I'm not going a step. It's too far from Peachtree Street!"

The consummate logic of that position very nearly convinced the police and the Lunacy Commission which later examined the old lady in Ordinary's Court. Odd she undeniably was. But insane? She obviously had a sufficient hold on her faculties to recognize one truth which is fixed and immutable in the minds of all clear-thinking citizens. And that, of course, is this: Only a lunatic would voluntarily and for any length of time leave Peachtree Street.

Why do we love it?

Not for itself alone, surely. There are more beautiful, more exciting, more interesting thoroughfares in the world. We love it because Peachtree Street symbolizes in our minds and in the minds of people all over the world a city called Atlanta, Georgia.

And why do we who for years couldn't get together on whether we are Atlantans or Atlantians (The *Atlanta Constitution* and the Atlantan Hotel insisted on the former; The *Atlanta Journal* and the Federal Penitentiary held out for "ian"), why do we lustily and with one accord proclaim Atlanta's superiority among the cities of the world?

The question engrossed Scarlett O'Hara back in 1862:

"Why was the place so different from the other Georgia towns? Why did it grow so fast? After all . . . it had nothing to recommend it — only the railroads and a bunch of mighty pushy people . . . Like herself, the town was a mixture of the old and the new in Georgia, in which the old often came off second best in its conflicts with the self-willed and vigorous new. Moreover, there was something personal, exciting about a town that was born — or at least christened — the same year she was christened."

To those of us who were born and christened somewhat later and who followed her onto Peachtree Street from older cities in the North, from small towns and farms and country places, Atlanta is the same — personal and exciting.

Its very newness is challenging. It hasn't had time to settle into any mold, to grow set in its ways. There's room for all, the kind of welcome that frontier communities must have held out to all new settlers: Come, bring your ideas and your energy to add to ours. Your tools, your axe and your shovel, your strength and your daring, your laughter and your learning . . . we can use you!

In a way Atlanta is even now, at close to 150 years old, a frontier town — the spiritual capital of what Henry Grady called and what continues to be the "New South." It is the last encampment of those who recognize the South itself as a still largely unexplored, undeveloped land. It has venturesomeness and the large tolerance of youth. It has confidence without the self-contained smugness of older, more insular cities.

Not so many years ago, *Atlanta Constitution* columnist Harold Martin, also an associate editor of the *Saturday Evening Post* and now a writer of history, thought up a brief and disarming answer to people who lengthily — and windily — disagreed with him. It sums up Atlanta's attitude toward both outside critics and those blessedly "pushy people" who move in with mighty ideas and monstrous big plans.

The answer: "Dear Sir, you may be right."

So often critics and newcomers have been right that it behooves Atlanta to be receptive of new knowledge, new talents, new money. At the time of her greatest travail, when her existence was spectacularly threatened by a torch-toting Yankee named W. T. Sherman, Atlanta entrusted to another Yankee — a New Englander named L. P. Grant — the task of fortifying the city.

Although the fortifications didn't stop Sherman, Atlanta recognized that the fault did not lie in the planning and the engineering skill of Colonel Grant, and in gratitude for his services and the acreage he contributed for it, the city named a park for him. (Visitors sometimes are misled into thinking that Grant Park may have been named for Ulysses S. Grant, but Atlanta is not *that* tolerant!)

There's nothing new about the fact that Yankee money has long made the economic wheels turn in the South. (Most of us Southerners grew up without knowing there was any other kind of money!) But Atlanta, unlike many older, more truly Deep South cities, does not take money with one hand and use the other to bar admittance to its more sacred social and cultural institutions.

Just as it entrusted its fortifications to a Yankee in 1860, today the custodian of our most cherished tradition and history is a citizen who happened to have been born in the North. Franklin M. Garrett, author of the most authoritative and comprehensive history of Atlanta — a hefty three-volume tome called *Atlanta and Environs* — was born in Wisconsin. For years the executive director of the Atlanta Historical Society was a gentleman named Colonel Allen P. Julian, who was born and grew up in Indiana. Wilbur Kurtz, the artist responsible for depicting scenes from

Atlanta's history in watercolor and technical adviser on the films, *Gone With the Wind*, Disney's *Song of the South* and *The Great Locomotive Chase*, came from Illinois.

The same happy acceptance of newcomers has given Atlanta the name among older southern cities of having a bumptious, nouveau riche society. Again Atlanta smiles sunnily and says, "Dear Sir, you may be right."

No matter what we have of money and breeding, society's most universally accepted commodities, nobody forgets for a moment that Atlanta also has Mrs. Mulligan.

According to history, Mrs. Mulligan was Atlanta's first arbiter of taste and manners. She gave the first party ever held in Atlanta and wrested and held for her day the leadership of Atlanta society.

Mrs. Mulligan was the wife of the foreman of one of the crews engaged in hacking a railroad right-of-way through the forest to the town which was in that year of 1839 called Terminus, forerunner of Atlanta.

Mr. Mulligan was considered a valuable man but he wouldn't stay on the job unless his wife joined him, and Mrs. Mulligan wouldn't set foot in the wilderness settlement unless the rough cabin assigned to her had boards put over its dirt floor. So the railroad builders, complaining at the loss of precious man and mule hours, took a team off the road and sent it miles to a mill to haul two loads of puncheons and laid Mrs. Mulligan a floor.

Mrs. Mulligan was gracious — Mrs. Mulligan was hospitable. She moved in and promptly gave a ball to which everyone was invited.

"It was a *crème de la crème* affair and the function established Mrs. Mulligan as the leader of the Four Hundred," John J. Thrasher, the railroad builder, later recounted in an interview with the *Atlanta Constitution*. "She was quite a fine-looking woman of strong physique and, if anybody had questioned her leadership, could have established her claim to the championship as well as the leadership."

Following Mrs. Mulligan's lead, the other railroad wives demanded plank floors for their shacks. The trapped railroad builders could but comply. Living conditions were improved, social activity was facilitated and the pattern for Atlanta society must have been set. For it continues true today, nearly a century and a half later, that spunk, spirit, resourcefulness and that Mulliganesque quality called personality hold their own handily anywhere Atlantans gather for any reason.

"Personal . . . exciting," Scarlett called our town. Latter-day chroniclers were inclined to put down as Atlanta's four chief claims to distinction a sheeted band of terrorists, a bottled drink, a great golfer and Margaret Mitchell's big book. They were commonly listed in this order: (1) Ku Klux Klan; (2) Coca-Cola; (3) Bobby Jones; (4) *Gone With the Wind*. Well, the KKK's so-called Invisible Empire hasn't been visible hereabouts in a long time. Ironically, this racist organization is not linked with Atlanta in the minds of most Americans as much as is the name of Martin Luther King, Jr., the slain civil rights leader who was born and is buried here, and whose home and memorial center daily attract hundreds of visitors. The late Bobby Jones, golfdom's Grand Slammer, is still revered, but he shares a place in the spotlight with another Atlantan, baseball's home-run king, Hank Aaron. The fame of Coca-Cola and *Gone With the Wind*, however, is not only secure, it has increased with each passing year.

These phenomena tell something about the town, to be sure. But they don't tell why it is personal and exciting to great masses of people who have only a passing interest in the heroes and heroines of the day, who never read *Gone With the Wind* and who drink buttermilk by day and bourbon and branch water by night.

I think it's the weather — the wonderful, terrible, capricious, never-the-same weather, brisker and cooler than anywhere else in the South or than in most northern cities because of its altitude (1050 feet), but moist and benign enough to nurture a green forest of trees and a year-round succession of blooming flowers and shrubs.

I think it is the poignant summertime fragrance of magnolias blooming in the parks and around Capitol Square. I think it's the smart, pretty, going-places look of the women and the way older men still take off their hats in elevators — even the fast, crowded, seventy-third-floor express elevators in the Plaza.

I think it's the young secretaries and Georgia State University co-eds tanning their legs in downtown Hurt Park at lunchtime and

the crowds that gather in the relatively new Woodruff Park at Five
Points to listen to a rock band or a street evangelist or a hoarsely
eloquent crusader for some cause. I think it is the big stores with
their escalators and fashion shows and their individual and strictly
local special events. From time to time Davison's, now called
Macy's after its parent company, tries its hand at growing potted
peach trees on the front sidewalk as proof that there *are* peach trees
on Peachtree Street. Or the crowds jamming Forsyth Street on
Thanksgiving night to see the lights go on on Rich's big skyborne
Christmas tree and to hear the carols sung from the store's glass
bridge by the town's biggest choirs.

I think it's a four-alarm fire on a winter night in a town that was
destroyed by fire once, nearly destroyed again and that remembers
with a sharp sense of tragedy the Winecoff Hotel holocaust of 1946.

It's Alabaster Alley in Buttermilk Bottom and Shakerag Road
and Coca-Cola Place and all the fashionable Northside residential
streets that got their names from grist mills or old Chattahoochee
River ferries. It's a rainy January and the General Assembly
convening on Capitol Hill . . . Noontime and history buffs spreading lunch on the old mossy tombstones in Oakland Cemetery. It's
the sound of pneumatic drills constantly, unceasingly tearing up
downtown streets . . . the shrill cry of a streamlined train heading
north in the night . . . the feisty yelp of a silver MARTA train
hauling commuters home . . . the clucking of a helicopter making
its shuttle run to the airport and the whine of jet airliners cutting
across the sky to the north, south, east and west.

It's a Georgia Tech football game on a Saturday afternoon, the
lifted boos and cheers of Braves baseball fans rising from a soup-
bowl-shaped stadium in the shadow of downtown skyscrapers. It's
an all-night gospel sing in the Civic Center, Big Bethel's white-
robed, golden-winged black choir, led by a Satan in red-satin tights
and cape, singing "Hand Me Down My Silver Trumpet, Gabriel,"
when they present the allegory *Heaven Bound* each year.

It's the Dogwood Festival, a St. Patrick's Day parade, a funeral
by Patterson. It's the way WSB used to sign off with "Dixie." It's
neck bones and pig tails and souse meat on sale at the Municipal
Market . . . the opulent, summertime richness of watermelon and
sweet corn and peaches and tomatoes at the State Farmer's Market.

Atlanta's Municipal Market has an international flair

It's traffic jams and parking tickets and policemen whistling like meadowlarks.

It's the memory of Roland Hayes singing the spirituals of his slave grandfather on the stage at Atlanta University, Carl Sandburg picking out a ballad on his guitar and Bessie Smith's "Down in Atlanta G-A, under the viaduct everyday . . . drinking corn and hollerin' hooray . . . " pouring out of an Auburn Avenue record shop.

Personal. Exciting. And something else that is paradoxical and very moving to me. Although for many years a disenfranchised capital city from the standpoint that Georgia's county unit system made the urban areas practically voiceless in state politics, Atlanta is a country town, a Georgia country town. Probably more than any other great metropolitan city in America (population two million, area 128 square miles) Atlanta draws its strength, its character and its flavor from the land.

Set a little north and west of the center of the biggest state east of the Mississippi, Atlanta has reared against the sky its tall buildings, pushing its industrial and executive parks out into seven adjoining counties; has crisscrossed the earth with railroads, a metropolitan transit system — part subway and part elevated — and millions of dollars of expressways; and has filled the air with the mighty roaring of winged traffic from Army and Navy bases, a jet bomber plant and the second busiest airport in America.

And yet it hasn't lost the oneness, what the old hymn called "the mystic sweet communion," with the red clay hills, the rolling fields and forests, the mountains and the piney woods, which gave it life. Certainly the economy has something to do with this. Despite the influx of industry in recent years, Georgia continues to be predominantly agricultural. Sales of forestry and poultry products total more than $18 billion a year. So it follows that what affects farm folks affects the folks in the capital city.

But I believe it's closer to the heart than to the pocketbook. I hear country in the speech of my neighbors — the turn of a phrase, the lapse into the quaint Elizabethan English of the hill country by a clerk in a store or a cultivated, Ivy League-educated guest at a party. I see it in the way Atlanta people trek to all parts of the state to participate in the old rituals and celebrations.

Camp-meeting time in Georgia was historically a season when crops were laid by and families hitched up the horses, tied the family milk cow to the back of the wagon and drove to Salem or Shiloh, Smyrna or New Hope campground for a week or two of spiritual refreshment — daily preaching and singing — and physical and mental refreshment — feasting and reunioning with friends and relatives. It hasn't changed much. Oh, the "tents," those rude shacks that usually encircle the open-air tabernacle of most campgrounds, may have acquired a coat of paint and an electric stove and refrigerator. And the wagon with the chairs in it has given way to a Cadillac or Chrysler. But Atlantans still go by the thousands to camp meeting in the summertime. Three or four of the old camp-meeting grounds flourish practically within the city limits.

Atlantans, as most Georgians, are predominantly Methodist or Baptist by upbringing and proud Bible-Belters all. And each summer you'll find many of them packing lunches and going back to the "homecomings" and the Decoration Days of the little country churches where they and their ancestors worshiped. While cicadas or the "July flies" make a summertime symphony in the oak trees overhead, these urban citizens spread dinner on the planks of rough deal tables with their country kin and wander about the old cemetery rereading the inscriptions on headstones, placing store-bought city flowers on the old graves.

Religion isn't all that ties Atlanta to the country. Anything that happens in Rising Fawn, Georgia, or Social Circle or Dewy Rose or Ty Ty or Talking Rock is news in Atlanta. Atlanta newspapers maintain a statewide network of correspondents and keep staff members on the road constantly covering the tobacco market in South Georgia, livestock and poultry production in Middle and North Georgia, rose queens and camelia queens and cotton queens and such improbably entitled belles as Miss Gum Spirits of Turpentine.

In the fall when the Blue Ridge Mountains blaze with crimson and gold, Atlantans go northeast to Hiawassee to the mountain fair to buy sourwood honey for their table and patchwork quilts for their beds. They stir up the dust on unpaved roads seeking out craft shows and syrup grindings and antique auctions. They rush to Gold

Rush Day in the old-time mining town of Dahlonega in the mountains and seek out Mule Days over the state where the intelligence and physical prowess of this still important farm animal is demonstrated.

Sure Atlanta has its country clubs, its symphony orchestra, its art galleries and, until recently, its annual season of the Metropolitan Opera Company. But its business and professional leaders still hold allegiance to Mary Mac's, a plain country-style restaurant where a cup of pot likker is likely to be the opener for a meal running heavily to turnip greens and fried okra, stewed corn and chicken dumplings.

It has a full complement of millionaires — the Coca-Cola kind and others. It has debut parties and white-columned mansions — antebellum atmosphere with postbellum air conditioning. An inland city, it has one of the biggest yacht clubs in America, but on their way to Lake Allatoona or Lake Lanier to play with their boats, members pass at the edge of the city limits the spot where until 1960 old Jim Whitley lived in a two-room log cabin in exactly the same way as his grandfather, who built it in 1840.

We have our nightclubs and foreign restaurants, our French and Italian movies. The town may have hooted derisively back in the 40s when "Ol' Gene" Talmadge grazed a cow on the lawn at the Governor's Mansion and invited his country constituency to drop by any time and share a pitcher of buttermilk with him. It was even satisfying to a lot of Atlantans to hear a rooster crowing and ducks quacking in the backyard of the new Governor's Mansion when Lester Maddox was governor. Some of those who laughed were pleased to accept an invitation to lunch from L. O. Moseley, the late manager of the old state-owned Henry Grady Hotel, on the days when he had his chef cook up a batch of chitt'lings or roast a possum.

Naturally the old lady didn't want to go to the State Hospital for the Insane because it *is* "too far from Peachtree Street."

She went — eventually. Such little eccentricities as foraging for food in garbage cans and catching rainwater to drink while hoarding $10,500 in cash on her person and twenty-five pianos she couldn't play in her house were certainly acceptable. But throwing rocks and those opprobrious words at children . . . *after all!*

Atlanta is notoriously mushy-headed about its children, holding them dearer than churches, Cokes and dogwood trees.

So the old lady went from Peachtree Street but not until after lengthy hearings in Fulton County Superior Court and not until considerable public sentiment had risen yeastily in her defense.

Margaret Mitchell, the little novelist who brought such renown to Atlanta, was one of those who gloried in the public clamor in behalf of the raffish old eccentric. It was evidence, she said, that her beloved hometown had not overreached itself and become a too-big city. It proved that Atlanta, small-town fashion, retains an affection and a tolerance for the independent, tough-minded, odd citizen who, in the country parlance, is "turned funny."

Struck down and fatally injured by a taxi driver, Peggy Mitchell has gone from Peachtree Street herself. And although her town has split its britches to become a big city, I don't think she would be disappointed in it. Atlanta is not only tolerant of the "turned funny" — it *is* turned funny. Individual, exasperating, sometimes ridiculous, it has all the endearing, surprising qualities inherent in the natural-born "character."

Love it? I'm crazy about it!

Everything's Peachtree

The young major who got on the plane in San Francisco had made the night horrible for the owl flight passengers. He was, as he loudly and unnecessarily assured everybody, "just a Georgia boy who will take a drink." With every mile his accent thickened and sugared like cane syrup cooked overlong and he noisily proclaimed his allegiance to Georgia in general and Atlanta, Georgia, in particular.

"Finest place on the face of the earth, and I ain't gon' never leave it no mo'!" he announced.

The two young stewardesses, unable to shush him, gave him a wide berth because the sight of them set up a lot of "Georgia-peach-you-all" talk which grew increasingly wearisome.

"A professional Georgian," the tired, gray-haired man next to me said as he punched his pillow and tried unsuccessfully to shut out the strains of "Ah'm a ramblin' wreck from Georgia Tech an' a helluva engineer!"

"Oh, he's just a homesick war hero," I offered placatingly.

"Maybe," said my neighbor, "but I bet a dollar he's from Ohio or Pennsylvania."

Sleep was impossible, so I volunteered to find out. The young man welcomed me with glad cries about Southern hospitality, apologies that he didn't have "ol' Gabe," the black butler, handy to serve me a mint julep and invited me to join him in heisting the University of Georgia's stirring, "Glory, Glory to Old Georgia."

Then I knew my seatmate was right.

A native Georgian is either a Tech supporter or a Georgia (University of) supporter, but never both. The man was filled with the kind of all-encompassing, loving kindness which is common to first-generation Atlantans and football fans who, poor things, had to go "off" to school. (Off is anywhere north of Vanderbilt or Washington and Lee.)

Before the first pale light of dawn presaged the coming day, the young major had made a manful confession. His benighted parents, a couple of rich but deserving midwesterners, had waited until he was fifteen years old to move to Atlanta. He had, for reasons beyond his control, gone "off" to school and then to the Army and overseas. But he was going to make it up. He was going to take his stand at the corner of Cain (now called International Boulevard) and Peachtree Street and spend the rest of his natural life "watching the Georgia peaches go by."

I comforted him as best I could by assuring him that he was practically a native son. Only twenty-five percent of Atlanta's population has the edge on him and me of having been born here. The rest of us have to make up for not being natives by being thrice-zealous converts.

The young officer went to sleep and I went back to my seat. My neighbor stirred drowsily and smilingly received my report. After a moment he said shyly, "If you're awake when we cross the Alabama line, would you mind punching me? I always like to be watching when home land is sighted."

I grinned and he went on defensively, "Maybe you haven't noticed, but from the air Atlanta is one of the prettiest cities in the country. All those green trees and the red earth. I just happen to prefer earth that's got some color to it, that's all. After all the pallid country I've been over, it's a relief to see land that's decently red."

I nodded solemnly and he turned his face to the window. Then he turned back.

"Uh . . . 1923 . . . from Michigan," he said.

The incident illustrates a couple of things about Atlanta: (1) the allegiance, sometimes tryingly loud-mouthed, of even her adopted sons; (2) the shiny-eyed pride with which settlers, both old and new, keep looking at the town. It is, I sometimes think, as if we were parents measuring with our eyes the growth and bonny bloom of a child.

Compared to older cities, Atlanta has perhaps a scarcity of tourist attractions. Even the most doggedly determined guidebook toter and plaque reader would be hard put to acquire aching feet or eyestrain "doing" Atlanta. This perturbs Atlantans not at all. We conscientiously tick off our "sights" for visitors — the Cyclorama, Stone Mountain, the Wren's Nest, a Minie-ball-battered gas streetlight which burns day and night, symbolizing the "eternal flame" of the Confederacy; Six Flags Over Georgia, the big dazzling amusement park west of town; offerings of the Atlanta Historical Society, which include a moved and restored pioneer vintage homestead, and a few others. But we don't really feel apologetic that our town's bag of tourist tricks isn't larger, any more than a parent can apologize because his beautiful, gifted, industrious daughter isn't also a ventriloquist and a tightrope walker.

We find Atlanta's workaday charms arresting enough. Any day of the week wherever strangers meet, at bus stops or in the breezy caverns of MARTA stations, in lounges or bank or post office lines, you hear the questions, "Have you seen . . .?" "Did you notice . . .?" It might be the opulent blooms and the trees leafing out in the giant-sized flower boxes in the Broad Street pedestrian mall, the face-washing they're giving the Henry Grady monument, the way the bulldozers are uprooting the woods around another beautiful northside estate or the newest downtown skyscraper.

We are a community of sidewalk superintendents, kibitzing enthusiastically at every hole in the ground, every convocation of helmeted steel workers, surefooted and lordly, high above our heads on the raw ochre ribs of a new building.

In the spring we are bemused by dogwood, the pristine dogwood, which edges streets and driveways with an immaculate ruching of starched blossoms and which stars rich man's garden and poor man's winter-drab backyard with whiteness. We organize tours and motorcades and stage (but never settle) side debates over whether this street in Druid Hills has a better show than that street in Ansley Park.

In the fall we busy about looking at the autumnal foliage which surely shows a wider range and a greater depth of color *this* year than ever before! Not so many years ago the Botanical Gardens Association of Fulton county held a beauty contest for trees and awarded metal plates to be attached to the trunks of the winners. This engendered a new kind of snobbery. People who would never think of bragging about their membership in the Piedmont Driving Club or that their daughter was Maid of Cotton bragged shamelessly that their sweetgum tree snagged top deciduous honors. An elderly West End widow of my acquaintance, who always considered that her banal bungalow was redeemed by the most glorious maple tree in town, was so miffed at losing "finest" to a Buckhead maple that she sold out, married a patent medicine salesman and moved to an apartment.

When interest in building palls (or in wrecking, which is a constant and equally fascinating show), when things are quiescent with the trees, Atlantans may shift their attention — but they're still looking.

This could be because a town so complex, so capriciously laid out, presents a challenge to the eye. It's so many different towns, tall upon the hills, sprawling along the Chattahoochee River, running underground on rails and granite-block streets, spilling over into neighboring counties. (The experts count seven counties as "core counties," but the metropolitan area clutches to its heart twelve or more.)

'Way back during the administration of Atlanta's long-time mayor, William B. Hartsfield, *Fortune* magazine endeared itself to the homefolks by calling the mayor one of the nine outstanding in the country and giving our town top place in areas of noise abatement and regional planning. More recently Rand McNalley rated it "the most livable city" in the country — a distinction which gladdened the hearts of the city fathers and all citizens who happened to notice. It was just as well that not everybody got giddy over the compliment because it was withdrawn shortly afterward. Pittsburgh, of all places, took top position and Atlanta slipped to a low eleventh spot. This was at a traumatic time in Atlanta's life, when a series of unsolved murders of black children gripped the entire populace with sadness and fear. In justice to Rand-McNalley, how could our town be called "livable" under the circumstances?

But that planning accolade was especially sweet to Atlanta ears because, although we're crazy about planning, spending many hours in committee meetings, zoning sessions and traffic engineering conferences, we have some of the most flagrantly unplanned streets in the world.

The downtown thoroughfares were once old Indian trails or cowpaths, winding leisurely along ridges, dipping down at springs and coming together at a swift-flowing artesian well which was drilled in the 1880's to supplement the town's water supply. The artesian well has since been plugged up; the flagpole which was erected in its place has been removed. A wide area in the middle is Five Points, where skeins of traffic are perpetually knotted and snarled, where most parades are reviewed, many civic campaigns are launched, and where Atlanta children used to go on New Year's Eve to hear firecrackers explode.

It is the nominal, although not the actual, center of our city and, of course, part of the language. A loudmouth is somebody who would "tell it at Five Points." A politician who has nothing to hide or, in the phrase given national coinage by President Eisenhower, a record "as clean as a hound's tooth," is one whose career has been as accessible to the public as Five Points. People have paid off their bets by trundling their opponents in a wheelbarrow through Five Points. The ultimate in public embarrassment, in raw exposure, is summed up in the phrase, "like being caught buck nekkid at Five Points."

Actually, Five Points is a sedate looking junction, as befits a financial section with banks and office buildings presenting a dignified facade. But a little of the old town pump atmosphere was restored to it when Atlanta's richest man and No. 1 philanthropist, Robert W. Woodruff, enabled the city to buy up and raze a couple of shabby business blocks and substitute a real people's park where something lively — and often loud — is usually going on, where birds sing and flowers bloom and there is a greensward and benches for resting and sunbathing. There's little tangible evidence, however, that this was the site of the first rude huddle of country stores in 1836, that where the tall William-Oliver Building now stands, Thomas Kile, grocer, had the honor of housing the first municipal election in 1848; that the First National Bank occupies the site of the old Jacob's Pharmacy where in 1887 a citizen with a headache turned Coca-Cola from a tonic to a beverage.

Only old-timers remember that here the horse cars loaded and unloaded, that a young lawyer named Woodrow Wilson passed here on his way to his first law office two blocks away, that Presidents have paraded here and such returning heroes as Bobby Jones, the grand slammer, have been welcomed here.

Sometimes somebody writes a letter to the editor bemoaning the passing of such Five Points institutions as Pitts' Cigar Store and Sweet Shop, which once faced Peachtree Street between Decatur Street and Edgewood Avenue. Pitts' closed in 1926, but the chocolate sodas he dispensed over his big square marble counter from 1894 to 1926 live on in memory.

Atlantans are prone to refer to the corners that jut out from Five Points as the points of a star — a figure which has been modified and carried on by city planners with Atlanta's expressway system depicted as a starfish, reaching out into a trade area of eighteen counties and drawing workers from a radius of a hundred miles.

But that is a planned star — or starfish — a product of traffic engineering with landscaped parkways and on-purpose greenswards and limited access. This other one, the one that chance and the moccasined feet of the Creek and the Cherokee laid off, is the one at heartbeat level, the one of teeming foot traffic, of intimate sounds and sights that are distinctly Atlanta.

Nobody agrees where Peachtree ends. Some mileage-minded people say it turns north a distance of seventeen miles, becoming in due course Peachtree Road and then Peachtree Industrial Boulevard, but I know Atlanta men who give smiling credence to the story which was told to them as little boys — that Peachtree Street runs to New York City.

Its beginning is more settled. A block south of Five Points there's a man-made island of green grass, towering magnolias and

Old and new mix in the view of Peachtree Street from Broad

blooming borders known as Plaza Park. At the edge of the park there's a peach tree and a small marker to inform the interested that at this spot the old stagecoach road to White Hall tavern ends and Peachtree Street begins.

Plaza Park was the city's first attempt to cover with beauty the railroad gulch, which runs under most of downtown Atlanta. Except for the ventilators that stick out at intervals in the grass and shrubbery, there's no sign that this blooming square is really one whopping dish garden and not just an ordinary park planted firmly on the earth. It may vibrate a little when trains pass beneath it, but that doesn't disturb the people who gather there to sit in the sunshine and to feed the pigeons. Salt from the pigeons' peanut and popcorn dispensing friends was the despair of the City Parks Department for years because it kept killing the grass. There was another problem, back before the department removed the fountain which splashed musically in that little square of greenness.

There were always phone calls the day after Halloween when some wag put bubble bath in the fountain and it sent beautiful, technicolor bubbles soaring dreamily through the chilled autumnal sunshine, breaking against dark old buildings, dipping in and out of traffic.

If you want a logical, overall, comprehensive picture of Atlanta, Plaza Park or of course Five Points is the place to start. At least that's what Atlantans say. Actually few local citizens have a logical, overall, comprehensive picture of our town. We get lost driving the cleaning woman home or trying to circle the block to pick up a friend in front of the library.

Atlanta, as many far travelers have observed, may be the only city in the world where it's possible to go around the block and never in due course return to your starting point. A standard, old settler joke about the residential section Ansley Park might well apply to any part of town. That's the one about the man who took a cat out to abandon him and then, hopelessly lost himself, had to follow the cat home.

But we've had our moments of trying to be like the organized cities and line up streets in a tidy fashion with numbers for names. Witness that small wedge of territory in the northeast section where the streets march along in numerical order . . . almost. Starting at

Third Street — don't ask me what happened to First and Second!
— they are resolutely numbered for maybe a dozen blocks before
wholesale skipping sets in. The number notion begins to go to pot
before you find Twentieth Street — and I don't think it's to be
found, but then I only lived in the neighborhood for twenty years
— and is abandoned entirely at Twenty-eighth Street.

This is confusing to orderly minds but doesn't upset Atlantans
unduly because where it's weak on consistency, it's strong on
Peachtree — and as any visitor to town for a day can't help
noticing, Atlantans like to call as many streets as possible
Peachtree. For example, part of what should have been Ninth Street
is called Peachtree Place; Thirteenth Street wears that number on
one sign and on another is designated as West Peachtree Park. All
in all there are thirty-odd streets with Peachtree worked adroitly
and not so adroitly into their names. A young reference librarian
trying to count them one day recently let out a cry of pure discovery: "Look!" he cried. "Here's one called Peachtree Blossom
Trail!" And there it was, indeed, old enough to be on a map in
suburban Gwinnett county.

In spite of this civic capriciousness and the Peachtree fixation, a
pattern does emerge, willy-nilly, for those who begin at Five Points
earnestly endeavoring to get some idea of how the town looks.

The five streets converging there are named Peachtree (of
course!), Whitehall, Edgewood Avenue, Marietta and Decatur.

Peachtree heads north through the better-looking business district, past the elegant Peachtree Center complex, an off-the-street
assortment of shops and restaurants near neighbor to such land-
mark hotels as the Regency Hyatt and the Plaza. It nips along
through many old and new community centers such as Tenth
Street, Garden Hills and Buckhead, crosses Peachtree Creek,
passes Oglethorpe University and the beautiful Peachtree Golf
Club with its antebellum clubhouse, and emerges at the edge of a
little town called Chamblee in a welter of gleaming new-style
industrial plants. Once famed as a boulevard of beautiful homes,
Peachtree now has more office buildings, apartment houses, condominiums, drive-in groceries and Dairy Queen bars than handsome residences. But it is the thoroughfare that cut closest to the
whole northeast and northwest area where houses like baronial

halls are set in the midst of wooded areas as tenderly clipped and groomed as parks.

Peachtree's other end, Whitehall street, meanders south through a busy section of chain shoe stores and dress shops, credit furniture stores, secondhand shops and eventually warehouses and transport truck terminals. It ends at the Central of Georgia railroad tracks, but if you cross the tracks and continue in the same general direction on another street, you come to West End, an old section gone shabby for a while but now in the process of restoration, where many prominent Atlantans once lived. (One of these citizens was Joel Chandler Harris, author of the Uncle Remus stories and editor of the *Constitution*. His quaint Victorian cottage, the Wren's Nest, is open to the public.)

Beyond that is Fort McPherson, headquarters for the U.S. Army Forces Command, the industrial-minded community of East Point and next door to it the tidy suburban community of College Park, home of the preparatory school, Woodward Academy. Nearby, a mile or so to the southeast, is the town of Hapeville and Hartsfield International Airport.

Back at Five Points, Edgewood Avenue heads southeast through a stone and steel thicket of office buildings. It passes the Hurt Building (named for a pioneer developer), Hurt Park, overlooked by the marble face of the old municipal auditorium but now a part of the big Georgia State University complex. Moving along, Edgewood passes the old Municipal Farmer's market, one of the older and bigger retail centers for farm products in the state, blocks of small stores and garages, many of them run by blacks. The main black business street, Auburn Avenue, called Sweet Auburn, runs parallel to Edgewood, once a tree-lined boulevard along which horse cars took such prominent Atlanta developers as Joel Hurt and Asa Candler to the town's first suburb, Inman Park. For a time this section of splendid old mansions was down on its luck, given over to seedy boarding and rooming houses, but a restoration project launched a decade or so ago has turned it into one of the more desirable — and expensive — close-to-town neighborhoods.

Marietta Street, the widest of the five thoroughfares, runs northwest from Five Points. It is the old route to Atlanta's smaller but older neighbor, the town of Marietta in Cobb county. A four-lane highway, built during World War II to handle traffic to the big Bell Bomber Plant (now Lockheed), was a faster, more direct route, and then Interstate 75, a multilane expressway, made even that look slow-poke. But old Marietta Street is busy with local traffic and colorful. From Peachtree it moves past the Henry Grady monument, the *Atlanta Journal-Constitution* building, the Federal Reserve bank, the main Post office and past the gates to the big new Coca-Cola company headquarters, which extends a block over to Luckie Street. Crossing railroad yards and the Chattahoochee river, Marietta Street enters Cobb county as the Old Marietta Road and moves at a slightly more leisurely pace through such pretty communities as Smyrna (the Jonquil City), the town of Marietta itself and eventually Kennesaw Mountain, where there is now a national park and battlefield museum and where Civil War historians gather to retrace the course of fighting leading up to the Battle of Atlanta.

That leaves Decatur Street of the five streets which converge at Five Points. Like Marietta Street, Decatur was named for the little town which was originally its destination. Now there are better ways of getting to Decatur in DeKalb county and beyond it Stone Mountain, but this street, like its glossier neighbor, Peachtree, once had other things to commend it than where it's going. Until it was slum-cleared to make way for the gleaming new buildings of Georgia State University, Decatur Street was shabby, rundown and enormously interesting. It was once a blues town, the home of the famous "81," the black theatre where Bessie Smith and her "Liberty Belles" got their start — a street of pawnshops and fish markets, of wholesale grocers and secondhand stores, of root and herb doctors and love potion merchants. There were overcrowded slum apartments upstairs over many businesses and at least one hardware store where you could buy kerosene lamps and iron washpots from a merchant who remembered when most of his customers came down from the mountains in wagon trains.

That old Victorian pile, the Kimball House, with its cupolas and squat little iron lace balconies, once the biggest hotel in the South, was on the corner of Decatur and Pryor Streets. Now the only reminder of it is a modest establishment, the Kimball House bar, where downtown workers, including many newspapermen, often gather for a light lunch or a homeward bound drink. In its day, the old Kimball House was the gathering place for Atlanta society, the place where visiting Presidents were entertained, the site of inaugural balls and political deals too delicate for transacting publicly at the capitol. In its final days, guests ran to transients or aging residents who either remembered its days of glory or hadn't much money and needed to do a little light housekeeping and perhaps keep a refrigerator in the hall.

The police station is also on Decatur Street. Grady Hospital is just a block off it on Butler. Slum clearance and that omnivorous monster, parking, razed blocks of old buildings, evicted pawn shops and peanut and fried catfish vendors. Even Hungry Corner, the traffic island at the intersection of Decatur and Central Avenue, no longer functions as the place where jobless laborers gathered to cadge a bit of casual employment. It has been displaced by labor pool agencies around town, perhaps more efficient but not nearly so colorful.

But the disciples of conformity haven't always won where these old streets are concerned. They have brought changes, it's true. They have shined up the image of Decatur Street especially. But so far they haven't changed their names — a bad habit with Atlanta's city fathers. The first recorded effort in that direction was in 1929 when someone proposed that Decatur Street and Marietta Street be called East and West Main Streets, respectively. Atlantans resisted that at the top of their voices.

"I'd as soon think of changing Frisco's Chinatown to 'Daisy Dell' or New York's Fifth Avenue to 'Sunnydale,' " cried Loyd A. Wilhoit, a columnist of that day.

Which shows you. For a young city with youth's enthusiasm for tearing up and remaking things and youth's eagerness to conform, Atlanta can be surprisingly stubborn in its loyalty to the old. Main Street, indeed!

Along Came Sherman

CHAPTER III

"You think we're crazy on the subject of Peachtree?" The old settler asked the question of a visitor. "Sir, I'll tell you something. This town was sired by an iron horse but its dam was a *peach tree*! Remarkable union, remarkable offspring."

The speaker picked up his cane and limped off the bus at the Capitol City Club, chortling appreciatively at his own joke and leaving the baffled tourist just where he was, leafing dispiritedly through Mr. Gilmore's Street Guide.

He didn't explain, but history does.

Even before a New Hampshire Army engineer drove that stake in the ground in 1837, marking the beginning of a new kind of American city — a lusty, brawling little railroad town — there was a peach tree here. It was a tough and brave peach tree which by some magic found its way inland from the cultivated orchards of the coast and came to bloom and bear fruit on a strange high mound on the edge of the Cherokee Nation.

So phenomenal was the presence of a peach tree in the wilds along the Chattahoochee River that from time to time skeptics have tried to explain it away by saying that what the Indians called "Standing Peachtree" was really just another big old resinous pine or "pitch tree."

If that's right, the soldiers who built and manned the fort there during the War of 1812 were even worse spellers than the War Department archives indicate, because they called it Fort Peachtree *at* Standing Peachtree and the road connecting it with Fort Daniel in Gwinnett County thirty miles away was named — what else? — Peachtree Road!

Because Atlanta is such a young town, a lot of its history has the freshness of word-of-mouth telling. Until 1903 George Washington Collier, who was here when the Indians were and long before the railroad men, could give eyewitness account of the early days. He was a plain-spoken old farmer who lived in the woods north of Atlanta for eighty years, long enough to see his fields and vast woodland acres become high-priced urban real estate. He died a rich man, leaving a large family of descendants to enjoy positions of wealth and leadership in the upstart town which had followed him to the woods, yapping at his heels and shattering his solitude.

A *Constitution* reporter who went out to interview him in 1894 quoted the old man as saying, probably irascibly: "Towns? Towns? Why, there were no towns here when I came. There was nothing except land lots and trails and corn patches. There was no money. There were no railroads, no papers. We didn't get the mail but once a week. There wasn't any business to do, much. The farmers just made their own corn and ate it for bread, that was all."

Wash Collier didn't try to substitute the unbelievable peach tree with the mundane "pitch" tree. He said he saw the peach. "Standing Peachtree was right where Peachtree Creek runs into the Chattahoochee — right where the pumping station is now . . . There was a huge mound of earth heaped up there, big as this house, maybe bigger, and right on top of it grew a big peach tree. It bore fruit and was a useful and beautiful tree. But it was strange that it should grow on top of that mound, wasn't it?"

Maybe the seed was brought in by some Indian trader circulating between the Cherokee and Creek nations. Maybe that stern-visaged old Indian fighter, Andrew Jackson, refreshing himself with a lunch from his saddlebag, dropped the seed there. Perhaps an Indian squaw had it in her small pouch of kernels and planted it along with the corn one spring.

Whatever the explanation, Atlanta was identified by a beautiful, fruitful tree long before Georgia caught the national railroad fever and sent right-of-way crews forth in 1837 to find the spot at which a state-authorized railroad, to be built south from Tennessee, could pass around the mountains and head for the rich cotton country and the seaports to the south.

The railroads came in, bringing a new kind of life to Wash Collier's woods and the isolated country where a farmer named Hardy Ivy had erected a log cabin and started breaking the land. Crews of Irishmen felled trees and cut through the hillsides and built fills to make way for the Western and Atlantic first and then the Monroe Railroad and, by the start of the Civil War, three other railroads, the forerunners of the fifteen main lines of eight systems which made Atlanta the largest railroad center in the South.

They threw up their crude shacks, their saloons and their rough country stores. All kinds of people followed the railroads, and it's no wonder that some of the citizens of Decatur and Marietta looked askance at what was happening at the settlement the railroads had spawned.

There were prophecies of every stripe, but two cherished ones are recorded in Franklin Garrett's *Atlanta and Environs* in his chapter on the 1830's. Alexander Hamilton Stephens, who was to become Georgia's beloved "Little Aleck," U.S. senator, vice president of the Confederacy and later governor, visited the southeastern terminus of the W. A. Railroad as a young man of twenty-seven. He is said to have looked on the near-wilderness and cried, "What a magnificent inland city will at no distant date be built here!"

The other prophecy is attributed to a Decatur citizen, Dr. Chapman Powell, who, unlike many of his neighbors, thought the railroad might be an advantage to a community instead of a noisy, dirty nuisance. To a colleague in the legislature who predicted that the terminus of the railroad would "never be any more than an eating house," Dr. Powell retorted, "You will see the time when it will eat up Decatur!"

Decatur hasn't exactly been consumed, but it has grown accustomed to finding itself referred to as a part of Greater Atlanta. By 1851 Atlanta was four times the size of Decatur and had taken a chunk of Decatur's DeKalb County to make itself a brand-new

county. With typical frontier thoughtlessness, nobody remembered to make note of why the name Fulton was picked for the new
county, and historians are probably destined to remain in eternal
disagreement. Franklin Garrett was inclined to favor Hamilton
Fulton, the chief state engineer who was a member of the first
railroad survey party, but after weighing the contemporary evidence he reluctantly concluded that the honor belonged to Robert
Fulton, inventor of the steamboat. Dr. N. L. Angier, a native of
New Hampshire, is credited with having chosen the name for the
new county, and historian Garrett thinks it likely that Dr. Angier
was more impressed by the man whose invention made the Savannah the first steamship to cross the Atlantic than by an obscure
railroad surveyor.

But there's no doubt where Atlanta got its name — from the
railroads, of course.

Called first "the terminus" and then "Terminus" and finally
incorporated under the name of Marthasville (for the daughter of
Wilson Lumpkin, one of the railroad builders and an ex-governor
of Georgia), the little town was rechristened Atlanta in 1845 in a
high-handed gesture from a railroad man.

Richard Peters, superintendent and resident engineer of the
finished portion of the W&A Railroad from Augusta to Covington,
had the job of announcing the opening of the road from Covington
to Marthasville and for some reason the name Marthasville didn't
suit him. Martha's father later said it was "the low voice of envy,"
but whatever prompted the change, it was no trouble for the
railroad to make it.

Mr. Peters asked the chief engineer, J. Edgar Thompson, who
was later to become president of the Pennsylvania Railroad, to
suggest a better name.

"Western and Atlantic," mulled Mr. Thompson. "Atlantic mas-
culine, Atlanta feminine. Eureka . . . Atlanta!"

The railroad adopted it, the town followed suit and the legislature promptly ratified it. Then everybody spent the next few years
explaining to literary-minded newspaper editors elsewhere that it
was Atlanta and not a typographical error. They naturally thought
the rambunctious little town must have been named for Atlanta,
goddess of fleetness and strength.

At any rate, Atlanta was on its way. The 1840's and '50's were years of almost phenomenal growth when the population, as one early visitor wrote, was "constantly augmenting." Even then, when its streets were red mud and roving livestock its main traffic problem, Atlantans were pleased with their town. Dr. George Gilman Smith, the Methodist minister and historian who came to Atlanta in 1847 as a child, quoted a bit of rhyme extolling the town's virtues:

"Atlanta, the greatest spot in all the nation,
The greatest place for legislation
Or any other occupation —
The very center of creation."

Oddly enough, this fulsome praise of the place stuck in his mind along with the recollection of typhoid fever as a fairly common summer complaint, the civic project to get the stumps out of the streets and the really precarious fight staged by law-abiding citizens to keep the town government out of the hands of a frontier-style underworld. Drunkards, gamblers, cock-fighters and idlers lived in Snake Nation (now Peters Street); Murrel's Row, a section of shanties on Decatur Street; and Slabtown, a community of huts thrown up on Decatur Street out of slabs from Jonathon Norcross' mill. These "baddies," organized as the Free and Rowdy Party, stole a small cannon, relic of the War of 1812, from Decatur where the townspeople shot it off on the Fourth of July and other celebratory occasions, brought it to Atlanta, loaded it with gravel and mud and opened fire on the store of the mayor, Jonathon Norcross.

Along with the litter on his front porch, they left a note warning him that if he didn't resign his post his store would be blown up. The mayor promptly issued a call for law-abiding citizens to rally. There were secret meetings on both sides, some hand-to-hand combat, but the villains were arrested, thrown in the log calaboose, which they promptly overturnd and escaped, and arrested again.

The communities of Snake Nation and Slabtown were burned down and what Dr. Smith called "vile women," who "visited their paramours in the daytime and without shame," were hauled out of town. (Franklin Garrett reports that they were taken "nearly to

Decatur," which, being but eight miles away, didn't exactly constitute complete banishment even in that day of slow travel.)

Dr. Smith, who reminisced about his childhood in a series of articles printed in the *Atlanta Journal* sixty years later, like a good Atlantan did not let any of the unfavorable aspects of those early days blind him to the innate charm of the place.

He wrote; "I never saw more beauty than there was in the springtime in the groves all over Atlanta. All the undergrowth except the azaleas and the dogwoods had been cut out. The sward was covered with the fairest woodland flowers, floxes, lilies, trilliums, violets, pink roots, primroses — a fairer vision than any garden of exotics show now. Honeysuckles of every beautiful hue, deep red, pink, golden, white, were in lavish luxuriance. The white dogwood was everywhere; the red woodbine and now and then a yellow jessamine climbed on the trees. When a stream was found, it was clear as crystal. I have seen few things so fair in this world of beauty as were the Atlanta woods in 1848."

Property values even then started climbing. Land on Peachtree Street which had been worth a couple of dollars an acre, when Hardy Ivy bought a land lot for $225 in garden produce in 1833, had gone up fast. By 1852 when a Massachusetts heavy machinery manufacturer (great grandfather of Robert Winship Woodruff, the late Coca-Cola tycoon and one of the richest men in the world) wanted an acre for a homesite, he had to pay $580 for it.

That particular acre happened to be where the Paramount theater was until 1960. When Mr. Winship was ready to sell it in 1866 after Sherman had been through, he was able to get $15,000 for it. Asa Candler bought it in 1909 for $97,000; Forrest and George W. Adair paid $120,000 for it two years later and in 1919 it was leased out for the building of the Paramount, valued at $625,000. The last time that little chunk of Hardy Ivy's old farm changed hands, it sold for millions.

The coming of Sherman, of course, was Atlanta's moment of high drama in history. The railroads which sired the town now shaped its destiny. As a transportation center, it was valuable to the Confederacy and therefore twice valuable to the Union.

The late Colonel Allen P. Julian, the Indiana-born secretary of the Atlanta Historical Society and curator of its museum for many years, used to joke that he was about to provoke a new intramural unpleasantness with his speeches contending that Atlanta, backed up by the rest of Georgia, was far more important strategically, economically and morale-wise to the Confederacy than any other southern city, even that one in Virginia. Citizens of Richmond gave Colonel Julian the most back talk, but anybody who really wants to make an issue of it is invited to drop by the Historical Society out on Andrews Drive, where the Campaign of Atlanta, which lasted from May to September of 1864, is refought almost daily, round by round, with the help of maps, photographs and stacks of documentary evidence.

Except for a solid core of experts in the Atlanta Historical Society, the Civil War Round Table and a few hobbyists who devote their Sundays and holidays to tramping over battlefields, the average Atlantan's idea of that great campaign is Vivien Leigh and Clark Gable and a great big noisy fire. Details of the battle, although highly regarded by military strategists near and far, are inclined to go fuzzy for native sons and daughters who have trouble remembering just where some of the picturesquely named hot spots of '64 are. Lickskillet, for instance, and Big Shanty and Rough and Ready.

Oddly enough, the people who can go to these places with the unerring instinct of homing pigeons, knowing that Lickskillet is on the west side, out Gordon Road, Big Shanty was the old name for the town of Kennesaw at the base of Kennesaw Mountain and Rough and Ready is the little community called Mountain View out near the airport, are often transplanted northerners turned Confederate.

However, when a local son or daughter takes up local history, it's surprising what a richness of material is available to make his study as interesting, as warmly personal as a tale told by a grandpa who was there or an old aunt who parched corn for coffee and defied Sherman's marauders from the smokehouse door. That's where most of the material comes from, of course — from the people who were there. Old diaries and letters and bits of family lore gave Margaret Mitchell her start.

Now new generations from the source, it is necessary for historians to sift more carefully the word-of-mouth accounts. Some stories have been beclouded by the passage of the years, some embroidered. The Atlanta Historical Society cautions students against believing that Sherman slept in the upstairs bedchamber and stabled his horse in the front hall of every antebellum house in the vicinity. This is a favorite story.

"If Sherman had slept everywhere in Georgia he is said to have slept," suggested Colonel Julian, "the war would had to have ended differently. He wouldn't have had time for any fighting."

Far from sleeping away that summer of '64, Sherman considered it a holy crusade to wipe out Atlanta as one of the enemy's chief military depots and manufactories and to "chastise a forward and erring people and turn them from following after false leaders and prophets."

It took him a while and he didn't quite pull it off single-handedly, since the Confederates themselves destroyed everything of military value with every inch of ground they gave. The National Cemetery at Marietta, with the headstones bearing the names of Ohio, Indiana and Massachusetts companies, attests to how much it cost him. And in spite of the bitter fighting, the shells bursting around them, the departure of the Confederate forces and the arrival of the enemy, many women and children and old men of Atlanta clung stubbornly to their homes until they were removed bodily by soldiers.

Students of the campaign usually begin at May 1, 1864, with General Sherman and approximately 100,000 well-equipped Union soldiers and 254 guns at Chattanooga, and the Confederate General Joseph E. Johnston and his fifty thousand not-so-well-equipped men and 187 guns fourteen miles south at Dalton.

Atlanta, eighty miles from Dalton, was Johnston's supply base and, according to Garrett, "full of machine and railroad shops, foundries and arsenals." Grant's instructions to Sherman that spring were to "move against Johnston's Army, to break it up and to get into the interior of the enemy's country as far as you can, inflicting all the damage you can against their resources."

General Johnston, with the familiar hill country and streams to help him, fought a defensive battle, which even his enemy, Sherman, found flawless from a military standpoint in the years after the war when such things were considered impartially. He held on to Dalton for twelve days and then retreated eighteen miles south to positions he had prepared at Resaca, where there was bitter fighting for a couple of days. But it was not all fighting, according to the old-timers who were there. At dusk, I have heard them say, the men of both sides settled in for the night.

"You could hear the bugler on the Yankee side start to play," an old lawyer told me. "He would play 'Yankee Doodle' and presently across the river you'd hear a southern boy strike up with 'Dixie.' And then as it got dark and the stars came out, one or the other of them would start 'Home Sweet Home' and the other would join in. They'd play along together in a way that made you want to cry — even more than all the shooting and dying in the daytime."

Johnston retreated slowly, and souvenir hunters today find in the fields and woods north of Atlanta sad mementos of such battles as the bloody four-day affair in Paulding County — the one Confederates identified as New Hope Church but which the Federals, whose losses were tremendous, called "Hell-Hole." There's a national park and museum at Kennesaw Mountain where tourists and Sunday picnickers sometimes drive in their station wagons and get the rangers on duty to show them how the battle lines were drawn, while the children look at the pitiful tattered old uniforms and have their pictures taken on the funny, old-fashioned little cannons.

Historians say that politics and no mistake of Sherman's was responsible for the slaughter of so many Federal soldiers at Kennesaw and at Cheatham's Hill. Lincoln, running for re-election, needed a Federal victory to bolster his policy of continuing war — and Sherman made the rash and ill-advised frontal assault in an effort to wrest that victory. That was on June 27, and less than a month later on July 17, politics on the other side, the Confederate side effected the replacement of the patient, watchful General Johnston with that colorful one-legged fighting man, "the gallant Hood of Texas."

Johnston, about to be flanked, had withdrawn from Kennesaw Mountain. The fighting was edging closer to Atlanta and the Confederate President Jefferson Davis and his chief of staff, General Braxton Bragg, were alarmed in Richmond. It may have been a strategic withdrawal, but to those men at that moment in history, it looked like the crafty, patient old Joe Johnston did not want to fight. The fact that he was out-numbered two to one apparently didn't matter.

General John B. Hood took over, and under orders to "turn back the federals before they reach Atlanta," he seized the offensive, hurled his tired, badly equipped forces at the enemy at Peachtree Creek and suffered a crushing defeat. A marble marker at Peachtree Road opposite Brighton Road commemorates the day, July 20, 1864, when 4,796 gray-clad soldiers died in defense of Atlanta.

The enemy's foot was on Peachtree Road and coming closer on the south and the east. The first shell had fallen on Atlanta, striking at the corner of Ellis and Ivy Streets and killing a little child.

From then until August 9, Atlanta was a city under siege, and yet strangely enough the citizens went on with life as usual. Some of them dug shelters in their backyards, and when the shelling was bad they sought refuge underground. The wounded were pouring into town and food and medicine were hard to get, but Samuel P. Richards, who founded Atlanta's oldest business, the Richards Paper Company, wrote in his diary on August 1, 1864:

"Nothing much of importance transpired during the week that we are aware of. We have had shelling semi-occasionally but thus far none of the deadly missiles have reached our house and we could look upon them at a safe distance with composure. For fear that they should ever reach us I have done several days' hard work preparing a pit in our cellar to retreat to for shelter. One shell pierced the top cornice of our store and went into Beach & Root's building opposite. . . . Our garden is helping us a great deal these hard times. . . . It is to be hoped the contest will not be prolonged indefinitely for there is nothing much to eat in Atlanta though if we keep the R.R. we will not quite starve, I trust."

Mr. Richards recorded that the shelling had ceased by August 25, and that there was a rumor that the enemy was retreating. "It is now known that they have deserted their camps around the city and are going somewhere, but what is their design is hard to tell. I fear that we have not yet got rid of them finally but they have some other plan in view to molest and injure us. But in the meantime we can rest in security for a while, safe from shells. . . ."

The Confederate grave section in old Oakland Cemetery

The reason for the let-up in shelling Atlanta was soon learned. Sherman's forces had put the Atlanta & West Point Railroad out of commission at Red Oak and Fairburn to the west of town and cut Hood's last supply line, the Macon & Western at Rough and Ready on the south side.

By 5 P.M. on September 1, Hood's army was evacuating the city, stripping gardens of every edible thing as they marched and singing the sad ballad, "Lorena." By midnight no Confederate soldiers were left except a few assigned to blow up the ammunition trains and destroy seven locomotives and eighty-one loaded cars — a job which took them five hours. (Movie demolition crews worked on it for weeks when seventy years later they re-enacted the scene for "Gone With the Wind.")

Mayor James M. Calhoun and a committee of citizens formally surrendered the city to Brigadier General William T. Ward, the nearest general officer, the next day, and within a week Sherman had settled in, setting up headquarters in the handsome, white-columned John Neal home, where the City Hall is today.

While the Yankee soldiers had taken over in Atlanta and were tearing down many fine residences to use the lumber to make Army quarters, Hood was hanging around outside planning to try to draw Sherman north again by striking at the W&A Railroad, which was now used to bring in supplies for the Federals. At Palmetto, a little town twenty miles west of Atlanta, President Jefferson Davis and two staff officers paid Hood a visit, reviewed the troops and were serenaded in the evening by the 20th Louisiana Band.

But Hood didn't succeed in drawing Sherman far from Atlanta. The wily Yankee firebrand left the Tennessee campaign to General George H. Thomas and returned to Atlanta to prepare for his march to the sea.

Before he left Atlanta, he ordered the destruction of what remained of the city's industrial and railroad plants. Four to five thousand residences, churches and stores also burned, either accidentally or by overzealous soldiers. Sherman's soldiers, well-provisioned, sang as they left Atlanta.

In his memoirs, the Yankee general told of riding out Decatur Street to the strains of the "Battle Hymn of the Republic" played by a 14th Corps band while the marching men sang, "John Brown's body lies a-mouldering in the grave."

A week later a state militiaman, sent by Gov. Joseph E. Brown to inspect the city, reported a scene of desolation. Thousands of carcasses of dead animals lay in the streets; rubble and ashes were all that remained of fine homes. Blackened stumps instead of shade trees, twisted iron fragments where there had been humming industry, the cemetery looted of small pieces of statuary, headstones overturned, coffins robbed of the silver nameplates and Yankee dead placed in some of the vaults!

A priest, Father Thomas O'Reilly, who had nursed the wounded and dying of both armies during the siege of Atlanta, had appealed to the Federal authorities and managed to save his own Church of the Immaculate Conception as well as four Protestant churches — Central Presbyterian, Second Baptist, Trinity Methodist and St. Philip's Episcopal. (All these churches were in the vicinity of the present City Hall at that time, but now only Father O'Reilly's Immaculate Conception, Central Presbyterian and Trinity Methodist remain. The others have moved out with the expanding city.)

These churches, some fifty families who refused to be evacuated (some of them northern sympathizers) and some very fine homes that mysteriously escaped the torch and "bushwhackers, robbers and deserters" were what Atlantans found when they began returning, almost before Sherman was out of sight, to begin rebuilding.

Miss Lizzie Perkerson, aunt of Angus Perkerson, who was editor of the *Atlanta Journal-Constitution* magazine for more than forty years, gave a vivid picture of life in the country that winter. In a letter to her brother, Angus, Sr., who was serving in the Confederate Army in Virginia, she wrote of conditions on the farm, which is still standing and is well within the city limits today.

"Pa's place has not got 200 rails [probably fence rails] on it, and not a building of any kind except the house and the old kitchen and smoke house. We have got one hog, four chickens, two old Yankee mules and ten dogs. . . . All our Negroes are at home and they are the only ones in the neighborhood. You can't imagine how it would take the Yankees down to see a whole gang of old Negroes and children go straggling along. We would tell them to look yonder are some of Sherman's reinforcements."

She reported that the homes of half a dozen of the neighbors were gone. She told of one, a doctor, whose family found a place to move in South Carolina and started. The second day out he fell off his horse — dead in the road.

"His family buried him by the roadside and went on," Miss Lizzie wrote.

"Cousin Mary and Will's children are at grandma's," she resumed the family news. "The Yankees burned Will's houses and took all the stock. Grandma says indeed she gave one of them three very good licks. He was taking the wheat out of the wheat house and the paddling stick was close by. She just put it to him.

"They all fear I am taking the fever now and I hope not. I feel very badly but I have gone through enough to make a stouter person than me feel badly. I hadn't undressed to go to bed in a month until last night. There has been a great deal of sickness in the country since the army came in here. But I don't think strange of it. The whole country is full of dead horses and mules, and the ditches standing full of stagnate water, enough to kill anything. We have but few soldiers in these parts now.

"The Yankees broke our loom all to pieces and burned it, but we have just got another one, and if we can get any wool carded we will make you some clothes yet. It is Ma's greatest trouble for fear you are in need and she can't help you."

Back in Atlanta, a writer for the *Daily Intelligencer*, which had refugeed to Macon, made a tour of the city and noted in detail the destruction, the roaming packs of half-wild dogs and a strange unearthly stillness.

But like Miss Lizzie, working at her new loom to make cloth to keep the winter cold from her brother fighting in Virginia, this Atlantan's story didn't stop with what was. He went on to what was to be.

"Let us now look to the future!" he wrote in the midst of death and desolation. "That which built Atlanta and made it a flourishing city will again restore it, purified, we trust, in many particulars by the fiery ordeal through which it has passed. Soon the whistles of the steam engines will again be heard. . . . Soon the cars from Macon and Montgomery and Augusta will bear their burdens into and through our city. Ere long, too, we feel

confident that the State Road will be in the process of reconstruction. . . . Let no one despond as to the future of our city!''

"We Are Coming to Meet You"

CHAPTER IV

"I attended a funeral once in Pickens County in my State. . . . It was a poor one-gallus fellow. . . . They buried him in the midst of a marble quarry; they cut through solid marble to make his grave; and yet a little tombstone they put above him was from Vermont. They buried him in the heart of a pine forest, and yet the pine coffin was imported from Cincinnati. They buried him within touch of an iron mine, and yet the nails in his coffin and the iron in the shovel that dug his grave were imported from Pittsburgh. They buried him by the side of the best sheep-grazing country on earth, and yet the wool in the coffin bands and the coffin bands themselves were brought from the North. The South didn't furnish a thing on earth for that funeral but the corpse and the hole in the ground. . . . They buried him in a New York coat and a Boston pair of shoes and a pair of breeches from Chicago and a shirt from Cincinnati, leaving him nothing to carry into the next world with him to remind him of the country in which he lived and for which he fought for four years, but the chill blood in his veins and the marrow in his bones."

Atlantans are extremely fond of that quote. It finds its way into print in one form or another at least once a year. The newspapers and the Chamber of Commerce are especially partial to it, and even school children looking for some way of measuring Georgia's business and industrial growth latch on to it for their essays and term papers with the rapture of prophets stumbling upon fresh truth.

To understand the message's appeal for Atlantans, the stranger needs to know about the man who spoke it on a December day twenty-nine years after the Civil War.

He was Henry Woodfin Grady, the ardent young editor of the *Atlanta Constitution* who first wrote and then, blossoming into an orator of renown, spoke of a New South — a region where old enmities were forgotten, where resources in men and land would be expended on something besides those one-drop despots, cotton and tobacco. He preached that economic betterment was the key to all the South's problems and that "waving the bloody shirt" and nursing old hostilities were profitless gestures. He visualized for that New South "her cities vast hives of industry, her countryside the treasures from which their resources are drawn, her streams vocal with whirring spindles."

Mr. Grady came to the *Constitution* by way of the University of Georgia in his native Athens, the University of Virginia and work on two or three other newspapers, including the *New York Herald.* He was but twenty-six years old when he joined the staff of the *Constitution* and in thirteen years he was to become one of the most persuasive writers and speakers in the whole nation. His friend and associate on the paper, Joel Chandler Harris, author of the Uncle Remus stories, was to write of him after his death: "His gift of expression was something marvelous. . . . Above any man I have ever known Mr. Grady possessed the faculty of imparting his personal magnetism to cold type."

Mr. Grady used these talents to plead constantly for a healing of the breach between the North and the South and to work to bring the three "I's" — investors, industries, immigrants — to the depleted land of his Confederate father, who was killed at Petersburg. Atlanta's four railroads were overtaxed by 1879 and Mr. Grady became fascinated by the prospect of bringing in new railroads. He visited all the railroad centers, made friends with the railroad barons of the day and spent the winter of 1880-81 in New

York writing and trying to interest northern capital in the South.

"I am firmly convinced that as soon as the South is firmly planted on her platform of liberation and progressive development and her position is well understood," he wrote back to the *Constitution*, "we shall see northern capital seeking southern investment with eagerness and the stream of immigration turned toward Georgia."

Mr. Grady's first major and most famous out-of-state speech was delivered in December 1886 at the banquet of the New England Club in New York. He began with an alleged quote from Sen. Ben Hill, some lines which Grady's biographer, Raymond Nixon, later tried to track down and found had been spoken by Hill but were improved immeasurably by Grady himself: "There was a South of slavery and secession — that South is dead. There is a South of union and freedom — that South, thank God, is living, breathing, growing every hour."

That speech, later called the New South speech, established Grady as an orator and as a "great pacificator," although he was not alone in these endeavors. He was invited back again and again, and in 1889 he stood before the Bay State Club of Boston and told the story of the poignant little "one gallus" fellow's funeral in Pickens County.

But only for contrast. For by that time Mr. Grady thought his Southland was well on the way to the new era he had worked for.

"Now we have improved on that," he said, referring to the necessity of importing all the "made" accouterments of the funeral. "We have got the biggest marble-cutting establishment on earth within a hundred yards of that grave. We have got a half-dozen woolen mills right around it, and iron mines and iron furnaces and iron factories. We are coming to meet you. We are going to take a noble revenge, as my friend Mr. Carnegie said last night, by invading every inch of your territory with iron, as you invaded ours twenty-nine years ago."

A few days later Henry W. Grady, not quite thirty-nine years old, was dead. He died at home on Peachtree Street December 23, 1889, from pneumonia. His death rocked Georgia and the nation. His friend Andrew Carnegie wired Captain E. P. Howell, publisher of the *Constitution*: "Only those who stood at Mr. Grady's side as we did and heard him at Boston can estimate the extent of the nation's loss in his death."

All over the country, newspapers headlined his death and the florid editorials of the day referred to him as the "apostle of the new faith," the man who "loved a nation back to peace," "an admirable illustration of that sagacious and progressive spirit which is gradually but surely renewing the South."

One of his neighbors and friends in Atlanta reduced the calamity of his death to more personal and intimate terms. "Our city is desolate," said Judge Howard Van Epps the day of the funeral. "We had some great public enterprises in view, that is, Henry had, and we were going to follow him, and overwork him as usual. We are disheartened — almost discouraged. Atlanta is so young and fiery, almost fierce in her civic energy and pulls so hard on the reins. Who will drive us now?"

The South as a whole might have needed the spur of Grady's vision and energy, but Atlanta, although missing him, already had the bit in her teeth. She was building, building fast and big.

Already a druggist named John S. Pemberton, who had led cavalry troops under General Joe Wheeler and moved to Atlanta after the war, was puttering around in the backyard with a mixture in a three-legged black iron pot which was to do more for the economy of the nation than Mr. Grady ever dreamed of in his visions of "vast hives of industry." Dr. Pemberton, as he was known, had been calling the stuff "French Wine Cola, the Ideal Nerve and Tonic Stimulant," and more or less dividing his attention between it and a couple of other homemade nostrums, Triplex Liver Pills and Globe Flower Cough Syrup.

The year Mr. Grady was making his New South speech, Dr. Pemberton fiddled around some more with his brew, taking out the wine and substituting a pinch of caffeine with the extract of cola.

While he was about it he also changed the name to one which may now be more familiar in some parts of the world than the name of the United Nations or even the United States: Coca-Cola.

Whether Dr. Pemberton's tonic did anything for the nerves is not known, but a favorite story in Atlanta is that it was very efficacious as a hangover cure and a queasy-stomach soother.

Asa Griggs Candler, who had come to town with $1.75 in his

pocket and taken a job at another drugstore, was too good a Methodist and too frugal to have hangovers. But he did have an uneasy stomach and he found Dr. Pemberton's brew so helpful that he bought the formula for $2,000 in 1891. Meanwhile, somebody had discovered by happy accident that a teaspoonful of the syrup mixed with charged water, instead of plain water, was a zippy drink, and Mr. Candler decided to take it out of the medicinal class and start peddling it as a drink for pleasure.

Local lore is full of accounts of how the Candler boys enraged the tenants beneath them in a building on Decatur Street by forgetting to watch the source of the family fortune — the Coca-Cola syrup kettle — and letting the sticky brown liquid boil over and run downstairs. Whether this is true or not, the boys watched their papa's $2,000 recipe boil into an asset which in 1919, while the old man was busy serving as mayor of Atlanta, they and other relatives sold for $25 million. (Mr. Asa Candler, Sr., did retain for himself one percent of his Coca-Cola stock.)

One of the three banks handling the transaction was local, the small Trust Company of Georgia, now known the world over as "the Coca-Cola bank." Ernest Woodruff was president of the Trust Company, and that is how his son, Robert, happened to give up the trucking business and become immersed in the soft drink business. The dominant figure in Coca-Cola management for six decades, Woodruff died in 1985 at the age of ninety-five years, having given an estimated $350 million to benefit medicine, education, social services and the arts. His was called one of the greatest success stories in American business, but little more than a month after Mr. Woodruff's death Coke management announced a change in the formula. Few stories beyond the declaration of war have set off a greater worldwide hullabaloo. So incensed were traditional Coca-Cola fans, so heated were their protests that after battling the opposition for three months, the soft drink tycoons called a press conference and threw in the towel. They would retain the new, sweeter Coke, all right, but they were returning to coolers and grocery shelves the old well-loved brew under the name Classic Coke.

In the one hundred years since it began — and Coca-Cola celebrated its centennial year with gala festivities in 1986 — the amber fluid which many Americans regard with almost patriotic affection has trickled fortunes in all directions.

Mr. Candler sold the first bottling rights to a couple of lawyers from Chattanooga for one dollar, which he didn't bother to collect. From this bottling franchise and others subsequently sold, numbering more than a thousand in the United States, multitudes of people have grown very wealthy. But for Atlanta children, growing up with a school tour of the Coca-Cola Company's home offices, there are two things almost more glamorous than money. One is that while on tour of the building, a very modern new building now, they can drink all the Coke they can hold without paying. The other is that somewhere in that building in a secret vault the priceless formula for the drink is said to reside. No matter what their parents say about the likelihood of its being in a sterile bank vault somewhere, children like to believe that the precious document is somewhere in that very building, the most golden of golden geese.

Mr. Woodruff had several homes — a New York apartment overlooking the East River in Manhattan, 30,000-acre Ichauway Plantation in South Georgia where he entertained such well-known visitors as President Eisenhower, and a 4,600-acre ranch near Cody, Wyoming, which formerly belonged to "Buffalo Bill" Cody. His principal residence was a Georgian residence on Tuxedo Road in Atlanta, a street lined with the homes of the Coca-Cola rich. The style of architecture varied, of course, but to Atlanta wags it is all "roccocola."

Sherman had barely got out of town and Henry W. Grady had not even arrived when another famous Atlanta business was started. Morris Rich, a small South Georgia merchant, borrowed five hundred dollars from his brother, William, in 1867 and opened a little retail dry goods store on Whitehall Street — very like one of those buildings you might remember from *Gone With the Wind*, a rough pine rectangle measuring a scant twenty by seventy-five feet.

According to store records, Rich's did $5,000 worth of business that year and had five employees. By 1986 there were nineteen Rich's stores ringing up over $700 million in business.

Until a year after the death of Richard H. Rich, grandson of the founder, in 1975, Rich's was mainly family run with such a colorful and unusual attitude toward its customers that department store scouts from all over the world came to study it. Legends abounded about Rich's return and exchange policy. Its credit policies were so liberal that it was a poor citizen indeed who didn't have a charge account there. Even the Chamber of Commerce used to have a fund of Rich's stories, telling delightedly the one about the woman who bought a cake for her daughter's wedding at Rich's and after it was eaten complained that the layers under the icing had been yellow instead of white. Rich's cheerfully gave her another cake — a white one. It was but one of many examples, and Atlantans gloried in them as well as the store's exceptional service to the community.

For example, back in the great depression of the 1932, Atlanta's school system found itself without money and was paying off the teachers with scrip. Walter Rich, nephew of Morris and cousin of Dick Rich, sent word to the authorities that Rich's still had cash in the till and the teachers could swap their scrip for it — no obligation. Hundreds of teachers and ex-teachers remember that gesture with gratitude and to all Atlanta it stands as proof of a special, we're-in-this-thing-together attitude at Rich's. The city later redeemed $645,000 in scrip from Rich's.

In 1943 the Rich's Foundation was formed for the purpose of distributing some of the big store's profits where they would do the most good. Recipients have included the Emory School of Business Administration, an out-patient clinic at Georgia Baptist Hospital, a grant to St. Joseph's Infirmary, a lab for the industrial engineering department at Georgia Tech, an electronic computer center at Tech, and radio station WABE-FM for the city and county school system.

Dick Rich's last act of notable community service — and he believed in it for all his employees — was to spearhead a drive to build a big memorial arts center in memory of a group of Atlanta art patrons who were killed in an airplane crash at Orly airport in Paris. Following his death the family relinquished control of the big store, becoming a division of Federated Department Stores. Many changes have come to the store, as with the city, but its policy of community service remains with sponsorship of such enterprises as an academy for high school drop-outs and a day care center for the children of working mothers, in which Rich's was joined by its downtown neighbors Atlanta newspapers, the federal reserve bank, Georgia Pacific and the First National bank.

Atlanta has many other department stores and shopping centers and malls, beginning with the bright and beautiful Peachtree Center complex downtown — enticing to those who labor in nearby offices and stores and those visitors and conventioneers at the neighboring hotels. South of Peachtree Center is another old Atlanta mercantile institution, now called Macy's but still Davison's to old-time Atlantans who knew it when. This store was established in Atlanta in 1897 and affiliated with the Macy chain in 1927. It was the first of the old Whitehall Street stores to move north a few blocks, "too far uptown," said the prophets of doom. How were they to know that "uptown" would within a few years extend into the wooded hills of twenty counties?

One of the first of Davison's branches was its small, chic beach shop on Sea Island. It remains notable to me because some years back I was assigned to cover the visit of Queen Juliana of the Netherlands to the Georgia coast. Since the queen was very shy and retiring, reporters saw little of her. Finally, hearing that her majesty had left her suite and was loose on the hotel grounds, I started looking for her. She was in Davison's beach shop buying bathing suits — size 48.

As a transportation and communication center, Atlanta first attracted businessmen with something to distribute. They shipped their goods in here to be relayed to all points of the southeast. Then it turned its hand to manufacturing with more than 2,700 manufacturers employing 142,000 workers. Lockheed's plant near Marietta — the largest aircraft plant in the United States under one roof — is the biggest employer in the state with jobs for nearly 15,000 people and a payroll which over a period of ten years runs into $748 million. This plant came to Atlanta in the World War II years as Bell Aircraft, known locally as "the bummer plant." General Motors and Ford are the next employers of numbers of workers. They are representative of the many northern concerns which started moving south even before the ashes had cooled.

However, the preponderance of Atlanta employers offers white collar rather than blue collar jobs, a service oriented economy. It is

A crane symbolizes Atlanta's constant building, rebuilding

A majestic new city rises from the treasured trees

the boast of Central Atlanta Progress, a non-profit corporation of business leaders, property owners and institutions working to build a better central city, that a total of 432 of *Fortune* magazine's "Fortune 500" companies, by all accounts the most successful in the nation, are located in Atlanta. Two of the biggest, of course, are Coca-Cola and Georgia Pacific with IBM close by.

The effect of all this brisk business activity has been incalculable for Atlanta culturally, educationally and politically. As the late Richard Rich was prone to point out, business involvement in all aspects of life in the city is in the Atlanta tradition. There are cities, he contended, where business and industrial leaders insulate themselves against the concerns of city government and grubby social problems. Political corruption and crime flourish in such places.

Atlanta business leaders have a long-standing habit of making themselves available to the mayor when he needs counsel, and after nearly eighty years of having little say in state politics, they now make themselves available to the governor as well.

The late James V. Carmichael, an enormously popular native son ran for governor in 1946, collecting the highest number of popular votes ever cast for a candidate in Georgia yet losing to Gene Talmadge because of the county unit system. He had little personal taste for politics but ran out of a sense of public obligation. Similarly he headed many business and civic projects, including Bell Aircraft, the forerunner of Lockheed, and the Atlanta Art Association.

"When people are poor, as we were right after the war," he sometimes said, "they have to devote their energies to scrabbling for food. My grandparents lived during Reconstruction days and they had their hands full trying to wrest a living from the land. When things ease up a little, the next thing people strive for is education for their children and an improvement in health conditions. And after that, if they've worked hard and succeeded a little, they have some time and a few extra dollars they can spend for things that give them pleasure — a little beauty in their lives, pictures, maybe, music."

Although there have always been individuals who could afford these things, as a city Atlanta began to attain that measure of security and leisure in the twentieth century — a trend Henry

Grady would have seen as highly practical. For with the influx of technical people, engineers, executives, all with good educational backgrounds, from cities all over the world, so-called "advantages" are of prime importance.

As Jimmy Carmichael put it, "They want advantages for their children — museums, a symphony orchestra, concerts, the theater. Unless the community provides such things, these people are not going to stay. They are an economic necessity."

They're Counting Our Votes!

CHAPTER V

Atlantans, being Georgians and therefore mostly southern and largely country, love politics. This may go back to the pre-television, pre-automobile days when there wasn't much excitement in the boondocks and branch heads except that generated by the exercise of men striving for public office. If there had been anywhere else to go, any other form of public entertainment, it's possible the rural southerner wouldn't have developed such a marked taste for oratory and barbecue.

Having little enough to divert them, however, at "lay-by time," when there was nothing to do in the fields except let the crops grow, and the summer protracted meeting had run its course, a political rally at the county seat was a welcome event. Men of all ages from bearded grandpas to shirt-tail boys saddled up horses, hitched the mule to the wagon or set out afoot to hear such spellbinders as fiery old Bob Toombs, Little Aleck Stephens, Tom Watson and, in later years, Ol' Gene Talmadge.

Even before they had the right to vote, the womenfolks frequently went along too, listening from the sidelines, minding the children, watching the hickory smoke curl up from the pits where a beef and several shoats roasted, laved in sauce and man-tended.

You have but to read some of the old speeches to realize that politics in Georgia for many generations was better than any road show. Tom Watson's "ideal goddess" — Eloquence — was everybody's. The conduct of public affairs evolved from a game that gentlemen played in the days of the Revolution to a game anybody could play, and the talented or lucky amateur frequently won.

Atlanta, which wrested the state capitol from Milledgeville in 1868, held for nearly a hundred years a strangely paradoxical position in state politics. It has offered the arena for the main events of the show.

Here is the State House, its gold dome visible from all directions, dominating, when the sun hits it, even a skyline of towering office buldings. (The gold for the dome was brought to town by wagon train in 1958 by the people of Dahlonega, the little town in the hill country where America's first gold rush was staged and the first U.S. mint operated. The mint was abandoned many years ago, but people still pan for gold and nearly every family had gold dust or nuggets to give for gilding the capitol dome.)

Here the General Assembly convenes, turning the town for forty days and nights into a churning, roiling cauldron of political activity — a watched pot. The hotels burgeon with senators and representatives from the 159 counties; traffic around Capitol Square is swelled by their cars. Restaurant and nightclub business booms. For a time it seems that every third man on the street is either in politics or wants to be.

In election years, the state campaign headquarters come to town and Peachtree Street takes on a carnival air with the banners of the candidates flapping in the breeze and soundtruck pitchmen roaming at large.

For his tenure of office, Atlanta is the governor's home. Until 1921 the executive mansion was on downtown Peachtree Street — a turreted Victorian, iron-fenced relic which the state replaced with the Henry Grady Hotel in 1924, moving the First Family to a gloomy granite architectural horror in Ansley Park. Now the glittering skyscraping Plaza Hotel has replaced the Henry Grady and there's a new governor's mansion at Buckhead.

The 1962 legislature authorized a replacement — a suitably white-columned mansion in the midst of acres of gardens on the

The dramatic and historic interior of the State Capitol

West Pace's Ferry Road site of the estate of former Atlanta mayor Robert F. Maddox. Built at a cost of more than $25 million, this official residence was quick to pick up life and color. Its first tenant, Gov. Lester Maddox, kept ducks in the backyard and rode his bicycle backward for the entertainment of tourists. Gov. and Mrs. George Busbee began their tenancy jolted by a tornado which caught the chief executive in the shower, uprooted trees and damaged the big house. They stayed two terms (Georgia law was changed to permit a governor to succeed himself), time enough to entertain His Royal Highness Prince Charles of Great Britain, who was their house guest for several days.

Georgians were delighted to hear that the Prince of Wales, an easy-going informal visitor, took off his shoes and walked around in his sock feet on one occasion. When he was ready to depart, he looked up the First Lady's mother, who was resting in her bed, and gave her a good-bye kiss on the cheek.

The present mansion is open to tours several days a week. The old Ansley Park house was not big enough to accommodate tourists, but the lighting of Christmas lights on the lawn and roof top was an annual fete which once drew automobiles loaded with children to the Prado. And occasionally something like an effigy burning or a student demonstration on the lawn made the nights lively.

In Gov. Marvin Griffin's regime, the neighbors turned out in their pajamas to watch Georgia Tech students burn the governor in effigy in protest to his ruling that Tech couldn't play a football team with a Negro on it.

Some neighbors still speak with amusement of the way the moving vans plied up and down like busy little tugboats before the governor's mansion in 1947. That was the year when Georgia had two governors at once — Herman Talmadge, now ex-senator Talmadge, contending by virtue of a write-in vote to be the heir apparent of his father, Ol' Gene, who was elected and died before he could take office, and M. E. Thompson, the lieutenant-governor who held (and was subsequently sustained by the State Supreme Court) that the right of succession was his. Ellis Arnall, the out-going Governor, tried to hang on until the courts settled the issue, and between the three of them moving in and out, the turnover at the mansion was something to see.

That's Atlanta, the capital city and the main arena for the state political show. But there's the other side — the Atlanta which politically was in the position of the well-known illegitimate child of the family reunion from the 1880's to the stirring 1960's. A unique arrangement of vote counting called the county unit system was responsible for this.

For generations students of government came to Georgia to behold democracy's anathema, election by the few, treated locally as a sacred tribal rite. Professor Albert B. Saye of the University of Georgia called it "the most disfranchised city in America."

The county unit system was born of the conviction that electing state officials and representatives in the U.S. Congress by popular vote would put political control in the hands of what Tom Watson called "a few city bosses . . . using corporation influence, the job-lash, money, whiskey and log-rolling." The rural counties were where virtue and honor resided, Watson and many of his successors firmly believed.

From the 1880's to 1917, the system existed informally, urgently defended and upheld by people like Watson. In 1917 with the enactment of the Neill Primary Act, it became law — a system whereby all candidates for congress, governor, state house officials and justices of the state supreme court and court of appeals were elected according to the number of counties they carried and not the number of votes they received. A candidate receiving the highest number of popular votes in a county was considered to have carried the county and to be entitled to the full vote of such county. The weight of that county's influence was measured on a unit basis, two votes for each representative it had in the lower house of the General Assembly.

Under that system, the smallest county in the state, little Echols in South Georgia, with a population of 1,876 people, had one unit representing 938 voters. Fulton County (Atlanta), with a population of 556,326, had six units, each representing 24,183 voters.

Naturally, the people of the cities, most of whom had come from the country originally, railed out against this disfranchisement, but it wasn't until 1962 that they had any real hope. When the U.S. Supreme Court ruled early in 1962 that the Federal District Court had power to grant a group of Nashville citizens more representation in the legislature, Georgia politicians — wrote *Constitution* political editor Reg Murphy — "knew the jig was up." Gov. Ernest Vandiver called the legislature back in to special session in the spring of 1962 in a bit of window dressing which was supposed to show the rural areas that the politicals still were fighting for them. But Vandiver and the legislature both knew well enough that they could not be successful.

While the legislature sat through the twelfth day of that grim special session, a three-judge Federal Court sitting half a mile away in the third-floor courtroom of Atlanta's old post office building began tearing into the system.

The legislature made minor concessions — a few more units for the cities. The courts said it wasn't enough. The state Democratic leadership decided any further granting of units to cities was impossible. The Democratic Executive Committee met and decided to hold the first popular-vote elections in about fifty years.

Ex-Gov. Marvin Griffin, making a bid for a comeback, panicked. He asked the committee to hold the election on a plurality basis, figuring a split vote would help him if there was no runoff.

The committee, dominated by the outgoing Gov. Vandiver, wouldn't have it. It said there must be a majority vote. Griffin's chances ended with that decision, but it wouldn't be proved until the hot summer's campaign was over and the votes were in on September 12. Griffin, a tough old veteran of the "hog-and hominy" school of politics and an arch-segregationist, was defeated by Carl Sanders, a young Augusta lawyer called a moderate by his supporters. (Sanders said of himself, "I'm a segregationist, but not a damned fool.")

The attacks on the county unit system continued. The legislature was pushed into another corner by a three-judge Federal Court decision during the summer, saying there must be reapportionment. The General Assembly came back into session in late September and boosted the Atlanta metropolitan area's representation in the Senate from one to twelve senators.

This brought on another election in a summer so election-ridden that people joked they couldn't go home to dinner any day until they had dropped by the polls and voted. Everybody got into the race for the Senate — old-timers in city and county jobs who hadn't dared to aspire to the state senate as long as there was only one seat, fresh young lawyers, housewives, Negros and Republicans.

When the smoke of battle cleared, Atlanta hadn't elected any women (one came close), but it had included in the round dozen the first Negro since the turn of the century, a lawyer named Leroy Johnson, and a white Republican, an insurance man named Dan MacIntyre, III.

For the first time in its history, the capital city had a respectable place at the council table in state leadership. The voices of the old-guard rural politician, viewing with alarm the political domination of "that silk stocking crowd at the Capital City Club," are still heard but they're growing fainter.

Actually, the rural resident had more chance of seeing the influence of Atlanta's "silk stocking crowd" than of the corrupt big-city bosses Tom Watson feared. Atlanta businessmen have historically taken an interest in government. One of the more famous instances was Coca-Cola magnate Asa Candler, who took office as mayor in 1917 to save the city from bankruptcy. He not only declined to take any salary for his services but he lent the city money from his private fortune to pull it out of the red.

Mills B. Lane, the colorful president of the far-flung Citizens and Southern National Bank chain, sent out postcards to sound out the electorate on the candidacy of another businessman, Ivan Allen, Jr., before the mayor's race in 1961. The town was going to be hard-pressed to find a successor to Bill Hartsfield, a man acceptable to business interests and at the same time dynamic and colorful enough to capture the imagination of the random voter.

Allen, a well-to-do second generation Atlanta office supply company executive, silver-haired, fifty years old, showed up well in banker Lane's poll, and he entered the race with the blessings of the Chamber of Commerce, Atlanta newspapers and a chunk of the so-called liberal and Negro vote. It was a five-man race and it wasn't easy.

Three of the contenders were old pros who had seen service in the legislature, the county commission or both. The fourth, like Allen, was an amateur, but what an amateur. Lester Garfield

Maddox, forty-five, operator of a fried-chicken emporium called the Pickrick, running on a segregation ticket with the support of White Citizens Council groups and, many supposed, the Ku Klux Klan, had all the color formerly associated with the old-school country politician.

He was sharp and feisty and funny but also alarming to a largely educated electorate, bent on economic and cultural progress. When he yelled that the election of Allen would mean that Auburn Avenue, the main Negro business district, "will run your city," voters raised in the Hartsfield tradition shuddered.

In the end, after a full summer of campaigning, a primary and a runoff, Allen swept to a decisive victory over Maddox.

Bill Hartsfield, the old campaigner, took over the microphone in the *Constitution* newsroom, where the returns were being tabulated and radio and television crews recorded the results, to praise Atlantans for once more choosing wisely.

For as long as he lived, of course, Hartsfield was "Mister Mayor" to many Atlantans. He held the nation's record for service as a mayor — more than a quarter of a century — and he has been named in many polls as one of the country's top municipal chieftains from the standpoint of achievement.

Caustic, witty, full of fight, it was characteristic of Mayor Bill that when he retired in 1961 he didn't sag down in a rocking chair or on a park bench somewhere and settle for being the city's elder statesman. He got himself a new wife, a new job, a new home — and he joined the PTA!

Some Atlantans tut-tutted when he filed suit for divorce from the first Mrs. Hartsfield, a shy, retiring woman who had been practically invisible to the public the thirty-two years of their marriage. Some of his contemporaries chuckled appreciatively that at the age of seventy-one he was eligible for the PTA. (The second Mrs. Hartsfield was a widow with a little boy.)

Come to think of it, his first PTA meeting could even symbolize something.

His successor, the new Mayor Allen, happened to be on the program. Although a man of social poise, Mayor Allen had not yet acquired Hartsfield's expertise as a welcomer, an opener, a ribbon-cutter and a shovel-handler at civic occasions. He stood up on the stage at R. L. Hope School and said he was "glad to be here at E. Rivers School."

Laughing but flustered herself, the principal said warmly, "Thank you, Mayor Hartsfield!"

I interviewed Mayor Hartsfield a couple of weeks before he went out of office and found him unable to keep his mind on reminiscences. Looking back did not interest him half as much as looking ahead. Besides, some of his recollections caused his adrenalin to flow so freely that he would be caught midway in a story and leap nimbly from his chair and give a blistering, devastatingly funny imitation of a detractor, a footdragger or an all-out opponent to some of his civic innovations.

Once Hartsfield was defeated — by a real estate/insurance man named Roy LeCraw and a margin of 111 votes in 1940. LeCraw had served but fourteen months when the United States entered World War II and he was recalled to active duty with the National Guard, in which he was a major. Hartsfield reclaimed the office with a sweeping victory over a field of seven other candidates.

But he learned something from that 1940 defeat. "I thought I did such a helluva good job I didn't need to campaign," he said. "But that's not right. You've got to fight every time! You could pave the streets with gold, reduce taxes to a nickel a year and scent the sewers with Chanel No. 5 and they wouldn't remember you unless you reminded them."

Although Hartsfield valued the voter, as only the successful politician can, he never let the desire for votes obscure his vision or dull the edge of his tongue when he felt the occasion warranted it.

There's a now-famous story of the time some movie press agents brought a trick horse into his office to receive the official welcome. The mayor hadn't known the welcome involved anything but a photograph and perhaps a pat on the nose for the horse, but when the press agent asked him to say a few words, he was by no means speechless.

"This is an historic occasion," he began with a fine roll of rhetoric. "It is the first time I've had the pleasure of receiving in my office a *whole horse!*"

The Darker Third

The talent for being surprised and gratified at themselves is nothing new to Atlantans. We have in us a large streak of the beldame who asked with classic self-astonishment, "La, me, can this be I?" We see ourselves as a plain and sturdy hen perpetually hatching ducklings.

As recently as the 1960's, when the laws separating the white race from the black race began to crumble, most Atlantans were truly amazed to find that there existed a whole community of wealthy, urbane and highly cultivated dark citizens in their midst.

Because of the presence of the big Atlanta University complex with its five associate institutions — Morris Brown, Morehouse, Clark, Spelman Colleges and Gammon Theological Seminary — just beyond downtown and the railroad tracks, they were aware that higher education for blacks was available and was attracting many splendid young people. After all, Atlanta University's president, the late Dr. Rufus Clement, had been elected to the Atlanta Board of Education by an overwhelming white and black vote.

Some members of the white business community were acquainted with what was known as the Big Four in Negro financial circles — Norris B. Herndon, son of a slave who started the family

The birthplace of Martin Luther King, Jr., on Auburn Avenue

fortune with a barber shop; Clayton R. Yates, a real estate developer and co-owner of the Yates and Milton drugstore chain; Lorrimer D. Milton, president of the Citizens Trust Company and partner in the drug concern; and Jessie B. Blayton, president of the Mutual Federal and owner of the Negro radio station WERD.

But what most Atlantans had not noticed was that down at the residential end of Auburn Avenue in a two-story frame house, a Baptist preacher and his wife had produced a little black son who was to become a world hero. His name: Martin Luther King, Jr.

The child had grown up there, playing around the neighborhood, climbing trees, attending black schools without anybody beyond the neighbors and his father's congregation at Ebenezer Baptist church paying much attention to him. It was known that he was bright because he had not yet graduated from Booker T. Washington high school when he passed the entrance examination to Morehouse College and enrolled there. A few months before his graduation from college, he was ordained as a Baptist preacher. His life moved along in a quiet, unobtrusive pattern for the next five or six years with his graduation from Morehouse followed by

Crozer divinity school in Pennsylvania, his marriage to Coretta Scott of Marion, Alabama, and his installation as pastor of the Dexter Avenue Baptist church in Montgomery. He had just received a Ph.D. degree in Systematic Theology from Boston University and come home for the birth of his first child in November 1955, when a strange thing happened on a Montgomery bus.

Rosa Parks, a forty-two-year-old Montgomery seamstress on her way home from work, refused to get up and give her seat to a white passenger. She was promptly jailed.

E.D. Nixon, a former sleeping car porter and head of Montgomery's struggling NAACP chapter, recognized it as a cause celebre that could bring about desegregation of public buses. He decided that twenty-six-year-old Martin Luther King, Jr., was the person to lead a bus boycott. According to the story, King didn't accept at once, pleading that he needed to think about it, but when Nixon called him back he said, "I've decided I'm going to go along with you."

The rest is history.

For the next thirteen years, Martin Luther King, Jr., led marches, protest demonstrations, was jailed, stabbed, confronted with police attentions with water hoses and police dogs, and made speeches about love and justice which were so eloquent they stirred a nation. His house in Montgomery was bombed once and a second bomb, unexploded, was found on the front porch a year later. Many of his followers died in hideous ways. Medgar Evers, a NAACP leader in Jackson, Mississippi, was assassinated at his home in the early morning darkness by a rifle bullet. Three civil rights workers in Mississippi were reported missing. Their bodies were discovered by the FBI buried at a dam construction site six weeks later. Mrs. Viola Liuzzo of Detroit was shot and killed while driving a carload of marchers to Selma. There was rioting with twenty-three people killed and 725 injured in Newark, forty-three killed and 324 injured in Detroit.

The King family moved back to Atlanta where Martin, Jr., joined his father as co-pastor of Ebenezer Baptist church, but he stayed in the front lines of the civil rights battle, organizing, marching, conferring with three presidents at the White House.

Desegregation was not his only cause. He deplored the war in Vietnam, speaking against it, urging again and again the philosophy of non-violence which he had learned in his studies of Mahatma Gandhi.

He "stirred the concern and sparked the conscience of a generation," said one writer. He changed the fabric of American life.

Atlanta police Chief Herbert Jenkins was one of those who foresaw Dr. King's death. The chief had been friends with Dr. King, Sr., for a long time, going back to the days when as a young policeman he was a driver for Mayor James L. Key. The mayor owed his election to the city's black vote and often went to meetings with black leaders. Young Herbert Jenkins had not known Negroes who were better educated, more travelled and better off financially than he was, and he was interested and impressed by those he met. Dr. King, Sr., and he talked often about matters affecting the black community and the chief saw young King grow up— "just another teen-ager," as he put it.

When civil rights battles began to be fought in Alabama, Jenkins saw the efforts of both the police from the state next door and the FBI to discredit the young black leader, to prove that he was not what he professed to be morally. On occasion they tried to enlist his help to prove that the young minister was foreign-born, an effort which amused the chief to no end. He knew that King was "under severe investigation" by the FBI, an organization the policeman admired and was accustomed to cooperating with, but didn't intend to "let 'em push us into doing any dirty work."

In Howell Raines' fine book of recollections about the civil rights movement, *My Soul Is Rested*, Chief Jenkins told about receiving a visit from Dr. King, Sr.

"They gon' kill my boy," the old man said.

"And I said," the chief related, " 'I think you're right, with the other things I've seen and heard.' "

A day or two later, Martin, Jr., and his father stopped in at the chief's office and the chief said he told him, "I don't have any ironclad information but I do pick up these little things, and I think you are in great danger. I think you're a marked man. I think if you don't leave Montgomery and come back to Atlanta, they gon' *bury* you over there.'

The younger King said, according to the chief, "You're probably right and I appreciate it. But I want you to know that this is my job, and if that's the way it ends, well, that's the way it'll have to end. I wouldn't stay away to prevent it, because I'm gon' do what I know I must do and let the consquences come."

The "consequences" they foresaw came on April 4, 1968, in Memphis when a sniper named James Earl Ray, hiding in a dingy room across the way, gunned down King as he stood on the second floor balcony of the Lorraine Motel talking to friends.

By that time Martin Luther King's eloquent voice had been heard around the world. The Voting Rights Act had been signed into law by President Lyndon B. Johnson, and Dr. King had gone to Norway to receive the Nobel Peace Prize. He came back to Atlanta to a big party thrown by the businessmen of the town at the Ansley hotel.

I attended that banquet at the invitation of our editor, Ralph McGill, not to cover it, particularly, although I probably wrote something about it, but because Mr. McGill happened to have an extra ticket. I didn't know then that the banquet had come close to being cancelled. I learned later than a large contingent of businessmen had turned reluctant, threatening not to attend.

The deciding voice was that of Robert W. Woodruff, the Coca-Cola magnate. He thought a homecoming celebration was mandatory, essential to goodwill and good manners. The business community fell in line.

It was a gala gathering, and many of those who were there were to remember for a long time the black man's "audacious faith in the future of mankind."

"I refuse to accept the cynical notion that nation after nation must spiral down a militaristic stairway into the hell of a thermonuclear destruction," he had told the Nobel commission. "I believe that unarmed truth and unconditional love will have the final word in reality. This is why right temporarily defeated is stronger than evil triumphant."

They brought Dr. King's body back to Atlanta, and hundreds of thousands lined the cortege route as a mule drawn wagon bore his coffin to the grave. Robert Kennedy, who himself would fall before an assassin's bullet two months later, was one of many prominent men and women who came to Atlanta to march in the funeral procession.

James Earl Ray pleaded guilty to murder. Accompanied by Mr. McGill, I had gone to Memphis to cover his trial, and I remember being disappointed that it was over in a matter of minutes after the elaborate preparations of the Shelby county sheriff's department to admit the press from all over the world and to assure an orderly trial. The *Constitution* had but one ticket to the courtroom, and I was touched that Mr. McGill, the old reporter whose fame had brought us that ticket (the *Journal* did not get one), said, "You're covering the trial, so you get the ticket. But when you have to file your story or go to the bathroom, I'll take the seat."

A few years later Ray would recant on his plea of guilty and go to federal court to try to withdraw it. I went back to Memphis to cover the appeal — alone. My old boss had died. Ray's effort failed and he was returned to prison.

Atlanta was probably the least turbulent of the big cities involved in the civil rights movement, and almost immediately its black leaders were turning to politics.

The day of Dr. King's funeral a young black lawyer named Maynard Jackson was at the hospital awaiting the birth of his first child. The solemnity of the "life-death cycle" engrossed him for long moments, and he made up his mind then that entering politics was the way to go for his country's good and for the future life of his newborn baby.

Jackson was a member of the "black aristocracy." His great great grandfather Andrew Jackson was a slave who bought his freedom and founded the Wheat Street Baptist church in Atlanta. His maternal grandfather was John Wesley Dobbs, a railway postal employee who despite being a Republican in a predominantly Democratic town was a power in politics and one of the "summit" Negro leaders who had worked diligently for the improvement of housing and health facilities for blacks long before the civil rights movement. He believed in education — higher education. One of his daughters, Maynard's mother, received a doctorate in French at the University of Toulouse in France and returned to this country to head the modern languages department at North Carolina Central

University in Durham. His aunt was the famed Metropolitan soprano, Mattiwilda Dobbs.

Born in Dallas, Texas, in 1938, Maynard was brought to Atlanta at the age of seven when his father became pastor of the Friendship Baptist church. He was graduated from Morehouse College at the age of eighteen and went on to obtain a law degree at North Carolina Central, where his mother taught, graduating *cum laude* and being designated as one of the outstanding debaters in the United States by the New York Bar Association.

His first bid for political office was almost a fluke. Twenty minutes before the deadline for qualifying, he borrowed $3,000 and entered the race for United States Senate against the powerful, oft considered invincible Herman Talmadge. He lost but not before piling up twenty-five percent of the statewide vote — a feat for an unknown black.

"Georgia has told the world," declared Jackson as he conceded defeat, "that any American — black or white, rich or poor, liberal or conservative — can run for public office in this state."

Spur-of-the-moment in his decision to challenge Talmadge, Jackson carefully planned his campaign for vice mayor of Atlanta — and he won with one-third of the white vote and ninety percent of the black vote. Next he went for mayor, entering the race in a field of eleven candidates, including the incumbent Mayor Sam Massell, Atlanta's first Jewish mayor, who had been elected as a liberal with the backing of blacks and the support of organized labor. Jackson was second in the eleven-man race and won the run-off against Massell with fifty-nine percent of the vote. He became the first black mayor of a major southern city and, at thirty-five years, the youngest in Atlanta's history.

At his inauguration in January 1974 — a gala in the Kennedy tradition with music by the Atlanta Symphony Orchestra — his aunt Mattiwilda Dobbs sang. She had previously refused to sing in Atlanta because the audiences were segregated.

Jackson served two terms and was succeeded by Andrew Young, a black preacher, son of a New Orleans dentist, who had been with Dr. King when he faced fire hoses and police dogs and was with him when he was slain. Young won by a landslide against the late Sidney Marcus, a long-time member of the Georgia legislature.

Young had helped to draft the Civil Rights Act of 1964 and the Voting Rights Act of 1965, and his name was well-known to Atlanta voters. Unsuccessful in a bid for Congress in 1970, he came back in 1972 and won, the only black member at that time to be elected from a predominantly white district, north or south. A Carter supporter, Young was called by the president "the finest elected official I've ever seen." He was named ambassador to the United Nations by Carter and is credited with having brought new luster to the United States with the African nations. Unfortunately, when he was found meeting with representatives from the PLO, the tide of public opinion against him caused him to resign, although the president had not asked it.

Nearly a quarter of century since Mayor Bill Hartsfield called Atlanta a city "too busy to hate," blacks have found it what Maynard Jackson called it, a city "*not* too busy to love." Blacks occupy many of the posts in the Georgia General Assembly and hold positions of authority in Atlanta from police and fire chief and sheriff to chairman of the school board.

It may not be what one writer called "a black Camelot," but it is a far cry from what they used to call the home of "the darker third." As of 1986 the population of Greater Atlanta was still predominantly white, but the city itself was sixty-seven percent black.

And the birthplace of Dr. Martin Luther King, Jr., almost alone among Atlanta leaders, has been designated an historic site, along with his grave and the memorial Center for Nonviolent Social Change, which has daily tours and a library where his papers are preserved.

Beginning in 1986 Georgia joined the nation in observing his birthday as a national holiday.

"More Normal than Usual"

CHAPTER VII

On August 29, 1961, the Atlanta Police Department's bulletin, a mimeographed newssheet issued daily to more than seven hundred officers, carried this announcement:

"In accordance with Federal and State regulations and under orders from the Federal Courts the Atlanta schools will be desegregated when schools open on August 30, 1961.

"If there are any objections to the manner and method of operation of the Atlanta Public Schools those objections must be made to the superintendent of schools office at City Hall and under no circumstances will objections, discussion or disturbance be permitted at any of the individual schools."

Very matter-of-factly the bulletin noted that "hate" literature would probably be distributed and that representatives of "hate" organizations might be on the scene. It listed the names and addresses of these individuals.

Toward the bottom of the page there was another list — the names and addresses of the Negro students and the schools each planned to attend.

A score card, a cop remarked later, "so we'll know the players."

But that wasn't all. The bulletin reminded the officers of their duty:

"The highest value of the law is the keeping of the peace. The Atlanta Police Department has full responsibility and authority to maintain the peace and good order over the entire city and especially at and around the schools."

The bulletin concluded by citing chapter and verse of that authority from local and state laws. It was signed by Herbert Jenkins, chief of police.

What happened in Atlanta on August 30, 1961, is now known throughout the world. The public schools were integrated peacefully. The next day newspapers all over the nation editorially hailed this Deep South city's "display of sanity and good sense."

The Police Department had planned and performed as their bulletin indicated they would — calmly, watchfully, meticulously "keeping the peace."

That bulletin, of course, was by no means the cause of Atlanta's peaceful school integration. It was, instead, the effect of a community attitude, of cumulative forces a long time abuilding.

There were times in the days leading up to August 30, 1961, when it appeared that Atlanta might have gone either way. To many old-guard southerners, breaking the traditional patterns of segregation was unthinkable. To some the very word "integration" was a dirty word connoting all kinds of hideous social evils, ranging from syphilis to consorting with Communists. Many people believed sincerely that if by any chance the South had not yet provided "separate but equal" schools, housing, health and recreation facilities for the races, it could and would, if let alone.

Two men knew better. One was an idealist, the late Ralph Emerson McGill, editor of the Atlanta *Constitution* from 1940 to 1960. The other was a practical politician, William Berry Hartsfield, who ended twenty-three years as mayor of Atlanta the first of January 1962.

McGill, long before the 1954 decision of the Supreme Court, had been attacking the inequities from the side of conscience.

"I wish those among us who are always so ardent in defense of their own interpretation of Southern traditions would be ardent in the defense of the Southern tradition which says that we always treat the Negro fairly," he wrote back in 1947 when the city spent fifty thousand dollars on a saddle ring for white citizens at Chastain Park and there was no park at all for Negroes.

"We don't and we never have given him a square rattle in education, before the bar of justice or in housing or in public parks. We have laws which separate the races but the same laws call for equal accommodations in facilities and transportation and we have cheated on that too. Yet if you begin to discuss such things, the clamor arises about 'social equality' and 'nigger loving' and the fearful run for cover."

Mayor Hartsfield wasn't so vocal about the rights and wrongs of the question, but he felt very strongly about what was good for Atlanta. From the time Negroes first began to push for small gains — members on the police force, the right to use city golf courses — when the mayor acted in their behalf, his political enemies might call him "nigger-loving" and the NAACP candidate, but the Negroes themselves knew better.

"Make no mistake," a Negro leader once said. "Mr. Hartsfield is by no means our Great White Father. He is simply a very practical man."

The mayor had no apology for that.

"When you stop to hate," he said again and again, "you stop all constructive work."

The golf course issue came up in 1957 with a U.S. Supreme Court decision. Mayor Hartsfield knew it would be invoked in Atlanta at any time and he got ready. He observed in cities where the golf courses were already integrated that relatively few Negroes played anyhow because it was a leisurely, time-consuming game. So he called a meeting of city parks employees to discuss the ruling and pointed out two simple home truths:

(1) If the court order was not complied with the golf courses would close.

(2) If they closed, one hundred white employees would lose their jobs and seventy thousand white users of the public links would lose a place to play.

Then in the courts he fought a delaying action aimed at one little known thing — to get the compliance date moved to the Christmas season.

"It's not easy for people to hate each other at Christmas time," he pointed out. "It's the time of year of universal goodwill. I couldn't believe we'd have any unpleasant incident then — and we didn't. "

Being both a practical and an imaginative man, Mayor Hartsfield took another little precaution. He called the Negro leader who had filed the suit and asked him not to begin his golf game at the time and the place announced where cameras and television crews would be assembled. It would avert a possible demonstration, he pointed out. The Negro doctor and his golfing companions agreed, and two days before Christmas they teed off on the city-owned Bobby Jones Golf Course without fanfare and without incident.

The desegregation of the city's trolleys went almost as smoothly, although in recognition of state Jim Crow laws the police had to arrest the hymn-singing Negroes who boarded the trolleys, Bibles in hand, and sat down on the front seats. Both sides understood what was going to happen, however, and a police lieutenant tells the story of one Negro would-be rider who got to the scene too late to demonstrate. He came panting into headquarters after the paddy wagon had arrived with the Rev. Williams Holmes Borders and his band of demonstrators and was so embarrassed to be left out that police obligingly locked him up with the others.

After the courts ruled, trolley integration went off without a hitch. But there were plenty of hitches elsewhere. Lunchrooms and restaurants in the department, variety and drug stores, normally the refuge of the downtown worker and shopper, closed right and left before the arrival of sit-in-throngs from the Negro youth movement. These were frequently joined by sympathetic students from the white high schools and colleges, which added even more to the ire of White Citizens Council members and similar white supremacy groups. Students picketed the stores, and on occasion the Ku Klux Klan, in full regalia but sans masks, which are prohibited by state law, picketed the pickets.

Through the intercession of the mayor and the Chamber of Commerce, this phase of the conflict ended with the integration of public eating places in the spring of 1962.

Through it all, however, the schools were at the heart of the conflict — all the schools of Georgia eventually, but the schools of Atlanta almost immediately.

U.S. District Judge Frank Hooper had already ordered the city Board of Education to submit a desegregation plan, and when that came back — a stair-step plan to begin with the twelfth grade — he ordered it to take effect in September 1960. Later he added the eleventh grade to that order. State law stood in the way and the legislature's answer was the appointment of a study commission headed by John Sibley, seventy-one, a prominent Atlanta lawyer-banker.

The commission collected opinions for many weeks, meeting in the cities and small towns of the state — and the majority of that opinion was that it was better to close the schools than to desegregate. Nevertheless, the commission's majority report recommended local option on the question.

Local option, as far as one group of Atlanta mothers was concerned, had to be swung to open schools at all costs. These were the women who were to later gain renown as the founders of HOPE (Help Our Public Education). They were a group of mothers who began by being horrified at having their broods at home on their hands all day long *if* the schools closed and went on from there to contemplate the long-range results of no schools.

Like Mayor Hartsfield, Mrs. Hamilton Lokey and Mrs. William Breeden, founders of HOPE, didn't waste any time hashing over the ideological aspects of segregation versus integration. They didn't even consider raising the question of how parents felt about sending their children to school with Negroes. All they wanted to do was to combine forces with parents who were determined to send their children to school, period.

Up until the organization of HOPE, the only people who were making themselves heard with any volume were the Negroes speaking through their court suits and such arch-segregationist groups as the Ku Klux Klan, the White Citizens Council and the newly organized GUTS (Georgians Unwilling To Surrender) and Separate Schools, Inc.

Now other groups began to be heard from. Ministers issued manifestos. There were three in all, signed by a total of several hundred ministers, white and black, of all faiths.

On Christmas Day 1960, in a special Christmas message, the ministers of the city said in part:

"We cannot ignore the differences which exist among us. It is not likely that we shall soon be fully agreed as to the specific steps which should be taken for the solution of our problems. We are convinced, however, that the only pathway to progress lies in the direction of friendship, of respect for the convictions of others and of determination to maintain communications between the leaders of all racial and religious groups within our community."

State leaders maintained their adamant stand against integration, however, until the event which shocked and horrified people in all 159 of the counties of the state: rioting at the University of Georgia.

Two Negro students, Hamilton Holmes and Charlayne Hunter of Atlanta, presented themselves to the registrar at the university in Athens on January 9 and were admitted as freshmen. Things were apparently going smoothly. They were assigned dormitory rooms and had started their classes and then darkness fell and the mobs gathered.

Local segregationists were joined by imported racists and rabble-rousers. Athens police and sheriff's officers were summoned by the university officials. The State Patrol was called out, rocks sailed through the air, tear gas bombs exploded. Inside the dormitories, girls from all over Georgia cowered in their darkened rooms, uncertain and fearful. The Negro students were sent home for a few days in the interest of peace while state officials pondered what to do.

It was a bitter cold night on Capitol Hill in Atlanta when the legislature convened in "unusual and emergency session" to hear what Gov. Ernest Vandiver had to say. He had been elected on a firm campaign promise that "no Negro . . . no not one . . . will ever attend a white school in Georgia."

If he adhered to that promise now the university would close, to be followed perhaps in weeks by the closing of schools in Atlanta and then elsewhere in the state.

The governor's wife and their three school-age children accompanied him down the aisle of the House chamber to the rostrum. They listened attentively to what he had to say.

"These past few days have been trying ones for all of us," he said. "Days of shock, frayed tempers, anger, shouts and even violence, but, over in the distance, through it all shone a steady light — the light of Georgia character, the innate, inbred integrity of our people."

A bit later he continued: "Having seen what can happen in the University System, we must move to protect the public schools and Georgia schoolchildren within the legal framework left to us. There is no — NO — sentiment in this state for a blind destruction of public education without offering an effective alternative. There never has been.

"Every legal means and resource to circumvent the effects of the decision, yes. Defiance, no. Private schools offered as a last resort, yes. Destruction of education, no. That has been the policy. That is the policy today. Our course is lawful resistance — not defiance — not violence."

Mandatory school-closing statutes were repealed, and a package of open-school bills was passed in their place.

The crisis was by no means over, but Charlayne Hunter (now Hunter-Galt, a public television anchorperson) and Hamilton Holmes returned to the University of Georgia where they proceeded in peace with their education.

In Atlanta the women in HOPE began promoting public acceptance of the change in tone from the state government. Out of this grew OASIS (Organizations Assisting Schools In September). It embraced fifty-three groups, ranging from civic clubs, labor unions, religious and business and professional organizations to Boy Scouts.

All over town OASIS affiliates held meetings to plan for desegregation. Community discussions were organized. Speakers and literature were provided, community leaders were encouraged to speak out and the campaign reached a climax the weekend before schools opened with "law and order" observances in churches. There were neighborhood coffees and PTA and garden club programs. The Society of Friends (Quakers) even arranged get-togethers for the white and Negro students who would be attending school together "to cushion the transition."

So on August 30, 1961, Atlanta became the first Deep South city to peacefully desegregate its public schools.

The scores of newspaper, magazine and wire service reporters and radio and television representatives who flocked into town, anticipating another Little Rock or New Orleans, might have been personally relieved but professionally let down at the outcome of the story.

Characteristically, Mayor Hartsfield, the old showman, turned it into an occasion to sell the charms and wonders of Atlanta to outlanders. Journalists from as far away as London might have trouble in years to come remembering the details of ten young Negro boys and girls starting to school with their white contemporaries in Atlanta. But they probably will never forget the fantastic handling of that story by the then mayor.

It was an era, remember, when newspaper photographers were having their cameras smashed by mobs. Reporters had their cars overturned, sometimes burned. Members of the press were often hurt. Later one was to lose his life in Mississippi. And nearly everywhere when all else failed, people blamed the strife on the presence of the press.

Contrast that to the Hartsfield reception in Atlanta.

The council chamber at City Hall was turned into a gigantic press room with tables, typewriters and telephones for all. Teletype machines were intalled for those who needed them. A radio system was installed for instant communication with the principals of each of the five schools and the officers on duty outside. Mayor Hartsfield, who manned the City Hall microphone most of the day, spelled from time to time by School Superintendent John Letson and Assistant Superintendent Rural Stephens, had but to flip a switch and the press was in communication with the people on the scene — able to ask questions and hear the answers. There was nothing to be gained by going out to the schools and constituting a crowd on a sidewalk, although most of us had a try at it. When there was a ripple in the smooth operation and there was a little one — the arrest of four teen-age boys who refused to move on when told to at one of the schools — the people in the council chamber were instantly alerted and taken to police headquarters to see the boys and to hear their stories in court.

Meanwhile in an anteroom to the council chamber, the Chamber of Commerce helped the visiting press to stave off starvation by setting forth snacks of Smithfield ham, hot biscuits, coffee and fruit juices and, of course, the ubiquitous Atlanta beverage, Coca-Cola.

Publisher McGill dropped by and Mayor Hartsfield introduced him as the South's "great man" and the architect of Atlanta's peaceable approach to its problems. McGill took a bow, remarking wryly that such fulsome praise was "what you get when you vote for Bill Hartsfield every time."

When school was out and the last piece of copy had been moved, buses provided by the transit company whirled up to take the guests on a tour of the city, with the mayor himself acting as guide. And they came back to a cocktail party whomped up in their honor by the merchants at the Biltmore Hotel.

H. W. Kelly, principle of Northside High School, inadvertently found words to describe the day so long prepared for. Asked at the radio-telephone press conference how things had gone at his school, Mr. Kelly remarked solemnly that as opening days went, that one was "a bit more normal than usual."

Atlantans, Proper and Improper

CHAPTER VIII

"Atlanta Society is like missionary stew," observed a long time member of it. "If you're in it, you know it. If you're not, you couldn't care less."

The shattering experience of an Atlanta woman who was in it and knew it offers another summation of Society-with-a-capital-S.

She went to a party at the home of an old friend — a party, specifically planned by the hostess to present her new daughter-in-law to the women who would be her mentors and her peers in her new hometown. This elderly guest was received, welcomed rather warmly, as befitted her status, introduced and was well into the petits fours when she remembered that she had promised to pick up a friend on the way to the party. Not wishing to interrupt her hostess, she slipped quietly out the back door, sent her chauffeur to retrieve the other guest and re-entered through the front door. Before she could explain, she was again warmly received, welcomed and introduced.

"My dear, she didn't even know I had *already arrived!*" this lady related, more in sorrow than censure. "It just shows you that Atlanta has grown so fast nobody notices any more where you've been, where you're going or *who* you are!"

Some old-timers will tell you it was ever thus in Atlanta. Since before Sherman, of the three — where you've been, where you're going and who you are — the greatest of these has been where you're going.

In the early days the fact that you came to Atlanta at all was a good indication that you were going somewhere. Those who didn't have energy and drive, spunk and ambition, stayed where they were — in older, well-established cities of the North and South. Even after Sherman's departure, those who came were often driven by another success-maker — desperation. They had nothing behind them except charred lands and burned-out homes or ruined businesses. They came for the express purpose of making good. Of course, those who got a head start promptly tried to impose the ancient probationary bans on newcomers. But even then the time was shorter than it is in most southern cities.

A story told about a member of the famous Nunnally's candy family illustrates that.

One of the Nunnally wives, herself both beautiful and well-born, was, according to the tale, showing a visitor about Atlanta and they passed the handsome Druid Hills mansion built by the founder of a big bakery and the father of a famous little cake which Atlanta children used to regard as a magnificent delicacy.

The visitor admired the house and inquired about the family until his guide felt obliged to tell him that they were rich but, since the father was a baker, socially inconsequential.

"What is the difference," mused the visitor, "between cakes and candy?"

To which the candy heiress replied with prompt and graceful good humor, "One generation."

A generation by some standards makes an Old Family in Atlanta. But the student of Atlanta Society must not overlook the fact that there are families who were here before 1865 and were bonafide, card-carrying aristocrats when they arrived. They had stature in that pushing, grabbing frontier era and they retained it after the war, when the rebuilding began, for any one of several reasons. They had come from sacked plantations or dead small towns seeking their fortunes, but they had grown up with "advantages" and had education, agreeable manners and some artistic

Roswell's Bulloch Hall, an antebellum mansion that survived Sherman

attainments. Or they were the near kin of men who had already attained prominence somewhere else in the professions, in politics or in war.

Frank Daniel, the Atlanta newspaperman who came from a small Georgia town and has been an interested and amused observer of Atlanta society for more than a quarter of a century, says he once knew a lady who was neither beautiful nor wealthy nor interesting. But she flourished on the Atlanta social scene nevertheless because, "*Both* her grandfathers were Confederate generals! She was absolutely impenetrable!"

This group might have become Atlanta's Society. Indeed, it *was* Atlanta Society for a while, establishing at least one still-prevailing rule for women who would succeed socially: Do good works.

The earliest Atlanta social leaders, unlike those in San Francisco, New York and New Orleans, weren't the women who gave the most elegant and interesting parties. They might have been practitioners of the art of fashionable entertaining, except that history took a hand. They hardly had time to raise white columns and get their magnolia and tea olive trees in the ground when The

War made ostentatious use of these homes not only bad taste but a sacrilege. Homes became hospitals for the Confederate wounded; such entertaining as went on was for the benefit of the brave men in gray. And erstwhile stylish hostesses became patriotically shabby, stripping themselves of their jewelry to be exchanged abroad for drugs and ammunition.

Not only did the town's nice women go threadbare and unadorned in early days, but when the fighting was over they went into the trenches and brought back and buried the unburied dead.

The first organization of the leading matrons of Atlanta was the Ladies Memorial Association, a body dedicated to preserving and decorating the Confederate graves and observing Confederate Memorial Day each April 26.

Naturally these ladies did not remain the town's social leaders — although the Association is still extant and active — any more than that small core of Old South aristocrats retained the helm of Society in general. Death vanquished the initial set, and although some of their descendants are still around and still prominent — bearing now the additional luster of Old Family status — many have fallen into obscurity or, worse yet, moved away, to be supplanted by newcomers perhaps more gifted than they at the twin arts of making money and making friends. The United Daughters of the Confederacy and the Daughters of the American Revolution, socially important groups in the beginning, now devote themselves to their original function of patriotic endeavor. Since the lifeblood of any capital-S Society is exclusiveness, the fertility of the fighting men of both wars cost these organizations their grip on Atlanta Society.

As one devoted member of both the UDC and DAR admitted plaintively; "How can we be *anybody* any more? There are so many of us! By now there must be millions of Daughters!"

But the pattern set by the earliest leaders in Atlanta — good works for nice women — survives. Atlanta Society has no idle rich. From the time they are young girls working in the Girls Circle for Tallulah Falls School until they make their debut at the Piedmont Driving Club, Atlanta women are caught up in Good Works.

This may take the form of one of the Junior League's many enterprises — the most impeccable, socially speaking, of all Good

Works. It could include membership on one or more boards of charitable organizations. (The A. G. Rhodes Home, a terminal hospital for the incurably ill, was founded by and continues to be operated by a board which started out as the Debutante Club of 1911.) It would most certainly include work for the Red Cross, Community Services or the Henrietta Egleston Children's Hospital, and either active work in or support of the Symphony Guild, the Music Club and the Atlanta Art Association. (The choice — work or support — naturally depends upon whether the lady has the more financial ability or physical stamina.)

Garden clubs like "the Daughters" are too numerous to constitute eclat in Atlanta, but because the first garden club in America was organized in Athens, Georgia, by the ladies of several distinguished, white-columned families, this organization enjoys rather more social prestige here than in many cities. And until they get so old and tired they seek refuge in apartment life, most Atlanta women feel obliged to belong to a garden club, usually their mother's. This serves the purpose of Good Works, in that the garden clubs keep beautiful many small parks and the grounds of charitable institutions and sponsor several flower shows a year. It also gives the beginning homemaker the confidence to cope with some irascible, darkskinned old yardman by whose side, if she is lucky, she will trudge through the autumns and springs of her middle years, spreading sheep manure, mulching camellias, and trampling out a vintage of glorious greensward and flowering borders.

Their devotion to Good Works has by no means made leaders of Atlanta society a bunch of lackluster bluestockings. As one delightful old lady, now in her seventies, explained after an evening of dancing the samba at the Capitol City Club, "Atlanta people love a romp. Always have. Surely you've heard of Lucy Peel?"

Lucy Peel, more frequently and deferentially referred to as Mrs. William Lawson Peel, died in 1923, but her name is still a legend in Atlanta. She was a ruling queen in Atlanta Society at the turn of the century and the author of a variety of civic causes, some of which were so impressive that the Chamber of Commerce once gave a banquet in her honor.

The only memorable thing surviving about that affair today is a story which Margaret Mitchell circulated joyfully in her youth. The official charged with paying oratorical tribute to Mrs. Peel became so drunk on his own eloquence or so captivated by the honored guest's charm that he finished off his address in this wise: "And in the future, Mrs. Peel, no matter what you do, remember, *the chamber is behind you!*"

Margaret Mitchell was, during her teen-age and debutante years, a pet of the older woman's, frequently regally singled out to serve in a sort of acolyte capacity in some of Mrs. Peel's Good Works.

They apparently had a great deal in common, Mrs. Peel and Peggy Mitchell, being bold and ardent spirits both. But the association suffered a severe setback when Peggy was commanded to get together some of her young friends and put on a program to entertain Mrs. Peel's adored Joseph Habersham Chapter of the DAR. Either wearying of the demands made on her or motivated by mischief, Peggy enlisted the aid of one of her more Bohemian cronies, dressed herself up like a Parisian strumpet and staged for the horrified Daughters a torrid apache dance.

It was precisely the kind of thing Mrs. Peel herself might have done in her younger days, but perversely — and probably because it offended her precious DAR chapter, which she truly loved — Mrs. Peel was monumentally outraged and summarily banished her young aide.

Ironically, Mrs. Peel herself is credited with having engineered a similar caper which produced pandemonium in Atlanta musical circles, put at least a momentary crimp in the career of Met Diva Geraldine Farrar and resulted in ministers mounting the pulpit to denounce the decline of morals among the upper classes.

Mrs. Peel and her husband, gentle, dignified colonel William Lawson Peel, who was president of the American National Bank, were among the early sponsors of the Metropolitan Opera in Atlanta. Out of a music festival staged in 1909 and starring Geraldine Farrar, a movement started to bring the Met to town. Miss Farrar herself gave impetus to the movement by confiding to a local gentleman who came to take her automobile-riding that an opera singer feels "stiff and constrained" performing without the costumes, scenery and acting opportunities of a Met production. "Why don't you people have the opera — the Metropolitan Company!" asked Miss Farrar. And Atlantans, led by Colonel Peel, who was subsequently renowned as "the father of grand opera in Atlanta," spun into action, headily wooing the Met into coming to Atlanta, replete with Enrico Caruso and a return engagement by Miss Farrar.

It was the beginning of a long-time love affair for Atlanta and opera — one which continued until the spring of 1986 when the Met announced the end of its road tours. But it hit a dilly of a snag in April 1920, thanks largely to Mrs. Peel.

Madame Farrar, essaying the role of Zaza in the opera of that name, had a mind to bring considerable verve and audacity to the role of the hoydenish sex queen. She thought the seductress might do a partial strip on stage and she sought counsel of Mrs. Peel to determine how far she might safely go with a Bible Belt audience.

"Go the limit," Mrs. Peel rashly advised her.

What Geraldine Farrar did that April day in 1920 might not horrify audiences conditioned to Jayne Mansfield and Marilyn Monroe, but it rocked Mrs. Peel's set. The singer not only took off a great many clothes essential to modesty, she flirted up her skirts and sprayed her teddies with perfume!

It was a great day for the men in the audience who had been dragged unwillingly to the performance. Never, reported the *Journal*'s O. B. Keeler, had Atlanta men dreamed that culture could be so exciting. But Atlanta women and Atlanta preachers were first stunned and then vociferous in their condemnation. Miss Farrar, reprimanded by the Met, blamed the Peels. A preacher, quoted in the *New York Times*, called it an arrant effort to inflame baser emotions and foretold for Atlanta a place in history next to Sodom and Gomorrah.

Geraldine Farrar never came back to Atlanta with the Met. Some years later she scheduled a concert appearance here, but it had to be cancelled because the church auditorium where the series was held was forbidden to her. Mrs. Peel, for once, was very quiet. She may have thought the whole furor senseless, she may have enjoyed it, and then again she may have been thinking about something else.

For although she was unique in many respects, Mrs. Peel was representative of Atlanta women leaders in her passionate espousal of civic projects. In a day when the Victorian notion that nice women didn't let their names be used in the newspapers was still prevalent, Mrs. Peel wrote several hundred signed newspaper articles taking the city fathers to task for the condition of the streets, urging increased recognition and use of Georgia products and campaigning for the betterment of highways and the construction of a Department of Archives to preserve the state's historical records.

Her literary talents were recognized by no lesser personage than the famed editor Henry W. Grady, who lived next door to the Peels. Grady frequently wrote his newspaper stories, editorials and speeches at home and then walked by and asked Mrs. Peel to read and criticize them. She was interested in history in general but particularly in family history and wrote three volumes of genealogy. She headed a society to raise funds for fatherless children of France during World War I and was state chairman of a National League of Woman's Service for the war effort.

Mrs. Peel was no beauty, but she was an arresting dark-eyed woman who wore magnificent dresses and hats. Her parties in the Victorian house at the corner of Peachtree and Forrest Avenue (now Ralph McGill Boulevard) were triumphs either of elegance or of informal high jinks in which she draped herself in an old curtain and romped through amateur theatricals with her children. The town's first kindergarten was organized at her house and the first theatrical group, the Players Club, met there.

Miss Isma Dooly, the *Constitution*'s society editor, extended herself to describe Mrs. Peel's clothes and Mrs. Peel's parties. She wrote of one reception which "almost surpassed the usual hospitality of this gracious home which is noted for the elegance of its entertainment." She described the food as "not only sweets and similar dainties but large platters of substantial delicacies like salads, pressed meats, the accompanying jellies, richly dressed cold dishes and several hot courses, all with wines."

"Mrs. Peel," she added, "who makes the wittiest of hostesses, was elegantly gowned in white satin, the coat effect showing a blouse of chiffon and thread lace."

But the time Mrs. Peel's gown attracted the most attention, *without* making the press, was the time she went to a large party in her shroud. The Peels had a white housekeeper named Jane Gregory, who came from the mountains. With the old mountaineer's distrust of Negro servants, Jane insisted on keeping all the family silver and food under lock and key. On the day of a party which she wished to attend, Mrs. Peel discovered that Jane had also locked up all her clothes. She had not only locked up the closets and wardrobes and hidden the key but she further complicated matters by suffering a mild stroke and taking to her bed.

The Peels' daughter, Marion, wife of Dr. Phinizy Calhoun, was giving a reception for members of Chi Phi fraternity, which was having a national meeting in Atlanta.

"Mama said she couldn't come," Mrs. Calhoun related. "She couldn't make Jane tell her where the keys were and she couldn't get at her clothes."

The party was in full swing, however, when Mrs. Calhoun looked out across the assembled guests and saw her mother sweeping regally in — a vision in a pink brocade dress she'd had stitched up to be buried in! Her family recognized it as the shroud she kept in a box in the attic and Mrs. Peel made no effort to deceive the other guests, some of whom still speak in tones of awe of the fascinating woman who waltzed the evening away in gala grave clothes.

When she died at the age of seventy-two, Mrs. Peel was, as she had planned, buried in the pink brocade with its blue bows.

Mrs. Peel has her detractors — men and women now grandparents who still smart at some snub or social defeat she dealt them in their youth. She was too outspoken and too contentious to be universally beloved. Her children and grandchildren found life with her strenuous, exacting and spellbinding. They couldn't bear to leave home or even to be sick because of the terrible risk of missing something. A sofa in the parlor was designated the "disease couch" because unless they were delirious or highly infectious, it was where every member of the family, including Mrs. Peel herself, chose to remain while ill.

Mrs. Peel had her organized charities and what her family calls her disorganized charities. She always kept an artist in the basement. They were practically always hungry and only occasionally talented, but in order to keep them busy, Mrs. Peel made the children and unresisting friends sit for their portraits.

She responded warmheartedly when she heard of trouble, although her generosity did not always take the most practical form. Once some distant cousins of hers lost everything they owned in a fire which burned down their home. Mrs. Peel sent them word to hang on and be of stout heart, she had help on the way. Very soon a great big box did arrive from Lucy Peel. The cousins hurriedly opened it to find she had sent them one dozen gorgeous plumed and flower-decked picture hats.

Mrs. Peel is but one Atlanta woman, more spirited than some, more dominant than many, but in a way representative of the Atlanta-style of southern society leader. A daughter of rural aristocracy whose father was the Confederate general Philip Cook, she had what was in her era, and still is, the approved background for this leadership. She came from the country, Schley county, by way of Wesleyan College and sojourns with well-placed cousins in an older city, Macon. She exhibited early what Atlanta has always liked — a nice blend of reverence for the past and hearty delight in the present. Gaiety and sociability pleased but by no means absorbed her. Her gifts were engaged in an arena larger and more important than the drawing room: the City of Atlanta, the State of Georgia, the economic, civic and cultural betterment of the region.

There were leaders before Mrs. Peel and there have been some since her, but the pattern remains little changed.

Miss Isma Dooly is perhaps the closest thing Atlanta ever had to a society editor-social arbiter. Miss Isma, assisted by her sister, Louise, and later by the delightful Bessie Shaw Stafford, ran the women's department of the *Constitution* from 1895 to her death in 1921. In a fluid, changing society, she was a fixed figurehead, and some of her readers came to depend upon her to decide who was and who was not Atlanta Society. For favored newcomers like William Randolph Hearst, who bought the Atlanta *Georgian* in 1912 and published it for twenty-seven years, eventually selling out to owners of the *Journal*, Miss Dooly sometimes determined the tone of a party by dictating the guest list.

But her interest went far beyond balls and euchre parties. She championed the organization of women's clubs as a means of tackling public measures. She developed what was new in the South — a sound woman's page of general interest, backing every measure involving welfare and advancement of women and children. She was especially interested in Negro children and poor mountain children, and she labored to get women admitted to the University of Georgia. A plaque on the first women's dormitory on the university campus and an auditorium bearing her name at the Tallulah Falls School for mountain children are testimony to the intelligence, energy and humanity of a magnetic woman who thought social betterment more important than Society.

Although she was no beauty and no belle, Miss Dooly attracted men readers and had many men friends, who enjoyed her conversation and were swayed by her convictions. Atlanta was very gay during the years when Miss Isma covered society, maybe gayer than it has been since. Telamon Cuyler, celebrated turn-of-the-century *bon vivant*, once tabulated the parties he went to during a seven weeks winter period. Just to contemplate his list is enough to make any presentday sit-by-the-television socialite limp with fatigue.

"I went to the following affairs, large and small," wrote Mr. Cuyler, and he listed: "Four cotillions, one bal masque, sixteen dances, one hop, one soiree, one question party, one musicale, nine evening theater parties, one matinee party, nineteen dinners, thirteen receptions, twenty-six teas, two stag dinners, four buffet luncheons, three Christmas parties, four eggnog parties, two children's parties, one surprise birthday party, two charity pay affairs, eight club affairs, four winter wheel (bicycle) meets, one New Year's party, one breakfast and eleven suppers."

Party-giving is rampant in Atlanta but it has taken a turn which might have horrified Melanie Wilkes in GWTW days. Big business sponsors many of the most gala and grander balls, all for the benefit of charity, of course, but, as one old Atlantan pointed out, all you have to be to attend is a person with the price of the ticket. The society department of Atlanta papers has shrunk considerably since the days of Miss Dooly. Yolande Gwin, a veteran on both papers, still holds the line, reporting annually on the fair young maidens who will "make their bow" at debut balls. But weddings, which once filled Sunday papers, slopping over into the dailies with many-columned pictures of bridal trains, have all but disappeared from the newspapers. Miss Gwin was heartened recently when management announced a change of policy. After banning bridal photographs for a number of years, it will now admit half-column cuts.

Members of Atlanta's Old Guard, in the fashion of Old Guard everywhere, look on their era as the halcyon days of Society. Sometimes over their whiskey sours at the Piedmont Driving Club, they speak mournfully of another time and another city. Sometimes, like one elderly, erstwhile belle, they play out renunciation scenes.

"Atlanta's not my town any more," this lady says, savoring nostalgia along with her bourbon. "The tackpots have taken over."

Tackpot may not be a term in the vocabulary of the New York, Newport or Boston hostess, but it is expressive enough for Atlantans. Taken from the root wood "tacky," meaning gauche and tasteless, tackpot designates the Johnny-Come-Lately, the district manager, the regional representative — the whole new segment of population that moved in from Illinois and Iowa and Salt Lake City to cause new subdivisions and schools and shopping centers to pop out like lightning bugs on a summer night; to join the old clubs or organize new ones, to give parties and go to them.

Far from being literal tackpots, some of these people are fully as charming and knowledgeable as the Old Guard — frequently more so. Their only impediment is one they themselves can't see — they don't remember-when.

"Peggy's Book"

CHAPTER IX

If Atlantans were to speak of "The Good Book," they would, in all probability, mean the Bible. When they speak of "The Book," there's no question. They mean *Gone With the Wind*. A cozy, more local name still in fairly common usage is "Peggy's book."

The querulous suggestion, sometimes voiced, that we make a good deal out of *Gone With the Wind* in this neck of the woods is no more true than the suggestion, for instance, that Carl Sandburg got hold of a molehill and turned it into a mountain of Lincolniana.

For the evidence is indisputable that *Gone With the Wind* was and is a phenomenon. It has been translated into twenty-seven languages, including the Arabic, copped most major literary prizes, including the Pulitzer, sold more than twenty-five million copies, and was made into a movie which even now, nearly fifty years after its release, is always playing somewhere in the world.

Margaret Baugh, the author's secretary, who until her death in 1967 kept nine-to-five hours in a downtown office handling correspondence with publishers in the far corners of the world and details of litigation against publishers in Iron Curtain countries who keep pirating it, once said of the movie, "It's like the former British Empire. The sun never seems to set on it."

A man in Denmark has two excursion boats named for Scarlett and Melanie, the heroines of the book. A publisher from the Netherlands came to Atlanta a few years ago expressly to put a basket of flowers on the grave of the author. Huntington Hartford, III, the Great Atlantic and Pacific Tea Company heir, telephoned from California one day a few years back to beg a sample of Peggy's handwriting to study for clues to her character. Hardly a week passes that the Chamber of Commerce is not asked for directions to Tara, Aunt Pittypat's house and Belle Watling's establishment or if Margaret Mitchell's home is open to the public.

All these tangible evidences that *Gone With the Wind* was a very special book are a source of pride to Atlantans. But even dearer to the home folks is recurring evidence that Peggy's book established a peculiar rapport between Georgians and people in all parts of the world. Wherever people have suffered war and subjugation, Margaret Mitchell's story of survival in the South has intensely personal meaning. It dramatized for citizens of sacked cities the world over that Atlanta was also a city — the only American city — totally destroyed by war and rebuilt.

Actually, for those earnest, admiring pilgrims who come to pay tribute to Margaret Mitchell and the GWTW characters, there's practically no physical shrine left in Atlanta. By Miss Mitchell's express instructions, her girlhood home was torn down. There is no Tara and never was one, except the movie set. A boardinghouse named for Aunt Pittypat on Peachtree at Fourth was torn down. The closest thing to Belle Watling's place is probably her modern counterpart in the oldest profession, the hotel with the girls "on call."

There's a grammar school named for Margaret Mitchell and a new street. Smith College Alumnae Club annually gives a scholarship in her name to some deserving Georgia girl. (The author herself attended Smith only a year and then came home to look after her father. But after GWTW she was invited back and awarded an honorary degree.) The Atlanta Public Library has a small room dedicated to her memory with an illuminated photograph of the author presiding over some glass cases containing a first edition and some foreign editions of the book, the little portable typewriter on which it was written, a sample of the manuscript and some still photographs from the film.

On request the visitor may get from an attendant in the adjacent Fine Arts Department a small booklet, brought out by the library in 1954, which contains a short biography of the author, an account of the book's publication and a story about the making of the movie. (These were written by William S. Howland, a former Southern Editor of *Time* and *Life* magazines and a long-time friend of Peggy's; Norman S. Berg, southeastern representative of The Macmillan Company, publishers, and Susan Myrick, an associate editor of the Macon *Telegraph*, who served as technical adviser on southern accent, manners and customs for the movie production.)

In the lobby of the *Atlanta Journal-Atlanta Constitution* building there are a couple of glass cases displaying pictures of Miss Mitchell as a girl reporter interviewing people like Rudolph Valentino, shots of the GWTW premiere and the small battered desk which she used when she worked for the Sunday magazine. Margaret Mitchell's passion for privacy and determination to leave no dusty shrines to be visited by people who never read her book was roundly defeated by the time *Gone With the Wind* was fifty years old. Atlanta and Jonesboro, spurred on by promoters of many commercial enterprises, staged celebrations, balls, parades and look-alike contests for which scores of handsome young people came out and did their darndest to look like Rhett and Scarlett. Three men came out of the west to dispute over which one of them played Melanie's baby, Beauregard Wilkes, in the movie. Apparently they all did, although it was perhaps the smallest and most forgettable role in the picture.

A man professing to have the world's largest collection of GWTW memorabilia put it on display. A woman opened up a kind of museum in the dilapidated old building where the Marshes lived when they were first married and which they called "The Dump." The *Atlanta Journal-Constitution* magazine where Peggy worked as a reporter put out a special memorial edition. (There was also one on the book's twenty-fifth anniversary.)

Reporters from all over the country flocked in to interview anybody who might have known Miss Mitchell. Yolande Gwin, veteran society editor who wrote the first review of "The Book," was a prime target. Betty Talmadge, divorced wife of former U.S.

Senator Herman Talmadge, drew network cameramen to her Love-joy farm, where she is in the process of restoring Peggy's grand-parents' old home. Puckish Betty was able to introduce them to a series of pets drawing their names from the book. Example: A goat named Billy T. Sherman.

Many books have been written about Peggy and many more about the making of the movie version of her book. Perhaps the definitive work is Anne Edwards' *Road to Tara*, which sold well but not a patch on GWTW even in its fiftieth year. A special commemorative edition vanished from bookstore shelves almost before the first GWTW parade was over and certainly before the last dance ended at any of the balls.

Perhaps Peggy would have been amused at this commotion, more likely annoyed. She went to great pains to arrange with her husband, John, and her brother, Stephens, to have her old home at 1401 Peachtree Street pulled down. I think she would have been widely amused at the way old clawfoot bathtubs, water closets, windows, mantels and paving stones sold when wreckers razed the 1912 house in 1952.

Her passionate distaste for having her private papers rummaged through by curious strangers or, worse yet, future biographers, led her husband to burn everything else she ever wrote and all but enough of the *Gone With the Wind* manuscript, notes and chro-nologies to prove her authorship of the book if it is at any time challenged. These are preserved in a very elaborate arrangement outlined by John Marsh in a codicil to his will, which was filed for probate shortly after his death, May 4, 1952. The papers were sealed in an envelop and locked in a vault at the Citizens and Southern Bank with a trust fund established to pay the rent on the vault and establish and authenticate Peggy's authorship of the big book if the need ever arises.

A curious provision of the will is that if Peggy's authorship is ever challenged and the envelop opened, its contents may go to the Atlanta Historical Society, if it is in existence, or the Public Library. If the papers are never needed to prove that his wife wrote the book and the trust is ended by court or governmental authority, "the papers therein shall be destroyed unopened" and the trust fund shall go to the Atlanta Historical Society.

Such a legal to-do over her work hardly seems in keeping with the picture most of her friends have of the light-hearted, outgoing Peggy. They attribute this legalistic policing of her privacy largely to her lawyer brother and her husband, an ex-newspaperman who became advertising director of the Georgia Power Company. But both brother and husband insisted that Peggy did not want her biography written or her unpublished works read.

Mr. Mitchell said she "probably wrote one or two novels besides *Gone With the Wind*. They were stashed away because for one reason or another she didn't want to offer them for publication. That's just a guess and I can't say whether they were written before or after *Gone With the Wind.*"

As a matter of fact, Peggy did not want to offer *Gone With the Wind* for publication. She wrote it between 1926 and 1929, let it lie untouched for six years, and even denied that she had a book when Harold S. Latham, Macmillan trade editor and vice-president, came to Atlanta looking for manuscripts in 1935. Medora Field Perkerson, an author who had been a colleague on the Sunday Magazine before she married their boss, Angus Perkerson, introduced Mr. Latham to Peggy with a cautious suggestion that he might ask about her manuscript. He did and she very "pleasantly but with firmness" got him off the subject, Mr. Latham related.

When she mentioned Mr. Latham's inquiry to her husband later in the day, he pointed out that she had nothing to lose by letting such a pro as a publisher have a look at her work. A few hours later, just before Mr. Latham was to depart for San Francisco, he received a call in his hotel room from Peggy. The sight she made, waiting for him in the lobby, must have been wonderful. She sat there, a little woman, overshadowed by a mountainous heap of smudgy, dog-eared typescript. Mr. Latham rushed out and bought a suitcase to pack the manuscript in and boarded the train.

Gone With the Wind was on its way.

The book came out June 30, 1936. The casting of the movie kept the nation in a state of argumentative suspense for a couple of years, and on December 13, 1939 — one of Atlanta's more memorable dates — the world premiere was held at Loew's Grand Theater. Slightly more than two thousand people got in the theater that night, but thousands jammed the streets to pay tribute to the little author, to Vivien Leigh and Clark Gable, the cinema Scarlett and Rhett, and half a dozen other Hollywood luminaries who came to town for the event.

Amazing fame and fortune had arrived for Margaret Mitchell, and Atlanta basked in it. To Peggy herself it made little appreciable difference. She and John continued to live in the second-floor apartment at 1268 Piedmont Avenue, where Margaret Baugh was already installed to help handle correspondence. Peggy, as a friend noted, seemed to buy nothing for herself except a fur coat and a secondhand automobile. But her gifts to others, given quietly, were generous and far-reaching. She dispatched hundreds of food packages to Europe during the war. As her devoted maid, Bessie Jordon, wrote of her after her death:

> She Fed the Hungry
> She gave drink to the Thirsty.
> She clothed the Naked.
> Shelted the out of doors.
> Ministered to the Sick and in Prison.

Personal charity, a concern for the ill and needy, had been a habit of life with Margaret Mitchell, even before the book brought her affluence. And although she was reared in comfort, the only daughter of a prominent lawyer, she had known lean days. She and John were married on the Fourth of July 1925, not quite a year after her unhappy, short-lived marriage (1922 to 1925) to Berrien K. Upshaw ended in divorce. John was in heavy debt as the result of a long illness and their combined salaries weren't impressive, but Peggy told her family and friends, "John and I are going to live poor as hell and get out of this jam."

Their first home was what Bill Howland called "a physically dark but intellectually bright" small apartment at 979 Crescent Avenue, just back of the Tenth Street shopping center, which they accurately referred to as "The Dump." It was here that she started writing on her book.

It was four blocks from "The Dump" — on Peachtree Street at Thirteenth — that she was to be fatally injured the night of August 11, 1949. An automobile driven by an off-duty taxi driver struck

Peggy as she and John started across Peachtree Street to see a movie at the Peachtree Art Theater. She died in Grady Hospital five days later. She suffered massive head injuries and never regained consciousness. The taxi driver, Hugh D. Gravitt, twenty-nine at the time, was convicted of involuntary manslaughter and sentenced to from twelve to eighteen months' imprisonment.

Two things helped to convict Gravitt of an accident which may not have been entirely his fault. After all, Peggy had apparently panicked while crossing the street and run into Gravitt's path because John, who stood still and waited, was not grazed by the car. But because Gravitt was photographed smiling when he was docketed at the jail and because he had a record of twenty-five violations, a public outcry which reached around the world sounded against him. The smile was wrongly interpreted to reflect the callous, unrepentant attitude of a killer.

Later, when he was serving time in the Bellwood Public Works camp, I talked to him and found him a desperately unhappy man who had been the victim of his own reflexes.

"A photographer said, 'Smile,'" he told me, "and I did it without thinking. I didn't feel like smiling. If I could I would have been the one in front of that car instead of the one driving it."

As for the traffic violations, they were no more than hundreds of taxi drivers pile up within a few years of hacking in downtown traffic.

As a matter of fact, Gravitt had been on his way to pick up medicine for his sick child when his car struck Georgia's most famous citizen — the beloved "little lady of the big book."

In the end, he served but four months, the requisite time on good behavior, before he was released on parole. But I have an idea that his life was permanently and irreparably scarred.

The deathwatch at Grady Hospital, the leaden hours of waiting in the hall for doctors' bulletins, was a sad experience for those of us who covered it. The funeral (admission by card for three hundred people, most of them old newspaper friends) was very moving. Peggy had been reared a Roman Catholic, but after her divorce and remarriage she departed the church of her childhood. An old friend, the Very Reverend Raimundo de Ovies, retired dean of St. Philip's Cathedral, read the simple Episcopal service in

Patterson's Chapel, asking mercy and peace for "thy daughter, Margaret."

Bareheaded multitudes lined the streets to the Mitchell family lot in old Oakland Cemetery, burial ground of founding citizens, but only a handful of flowers graced her coffin. These were roses grown within the walls of Atlanta Penitentiary by her old friends, the prisoners, to whom she had written, spoken and given prizes for literary efforts. At the family's request all others who might have sent flowers instead sent contributions for the treatment of the indigent at Grady Hospital.

It was a time of statewide mourning in Georgia. By order of the then-governor Herman Talmadge, the flag over the capitol flew at half-staff. But from my relatively short acquaintance with the blithe and bumptious little author, I think she may have been pleased that I didn't emerge from her injury and death without one bright patch of humor to remember.

It was a day or so after the funeral that Frank Daniel, the *Journal* reporter and a long-time friend of the Marshes, and I happened to meet at their apartment in quest of follow-up stories for our respective Sunday papers. (This was before the merger.)

John received us graciously and talked freely. But he was a very deliberate man, given to slow speech and rambling reminiscence. Each of us had questions to ask and were urgently conscious of our deadlines bearing down on us. John seemed to me to take an agonizingly long time with many interminable digressions, and when we finally got the information we came for, Frank and I bolted for the door together.

Outside, mindful of the fact that he was a much older and closer friend of our bereaved host, I daringly remarked that John Marsh was a very long-winded man.

"Yes," said Frank cheerfully. "I always said that Peggy's book, long as it was, was just a snappy comeback to something John had said."

From Whistle to White Mice

Sometimes Atlanta doctors, meeting in their handsome Academy of Medicine of West Peachtree Street, make a small bow in the direction of the portrait of a dark-eyed gentleman with whimsical eyes and a high starched collar.

Dr. Joshua Gilbert was their professional ancestor, Atlanta's first doctor — a man whose principal equipment in ministering to a town of five hundred people consisted of a horse, a whistle, a supply of quinine and his own indomitable determination to cure the sick.

Dr. Gilbert came here from South Carolina in 1845, when the town was still called Marthasville, and he stayed until his death in 1889. For a time he was the only doctor and so busy he blew a whistle on his rounds to let people know he was coming. The sound of that little whistle, shrilling night and day, alerted those who might need a doctor and they rushed out to stop him.

Sometimes in his haste he heard their complaints and prescribed without even getting off his horse — literally a horseback diagnosis. He rolled his own pills, kept no books, collected no accounts and pushed himself so hard his descendants tell of a particularly bitter winter when he almost froze to his saddle and a Negro servant had to pry him loose.

Dr. Gilbert was the forerunner of thousands of doctors, nurses, technicians and researchers who were to make Atlanta a leading, and in some instances unique, medical center in the nation.

That little whistle which must have comforted people in frontier days, reminding even the well that help was near if they needed it, has been succeeded by dozens of general and special hospitals, nearly five thousand doctors in the five county area, two medical schools and the U.S. Public Health Service's amazing Centers for Disease Control, which in 1986 observed its fortieth anniversary as the watchdog of the health of the nation. The CDC is the only major federal agency with headquarters outside metropolitan Washington, D.C., and over the last four decades, it has grown from obscurity into a complex of five federal centers and the National Institute for Occupational Safety and Health. Its staff has increased from 369 to 4,278 and its budget has grown from $1 million to $452 million.

Malaria brought the first little office and laboratories of the CDC to Atlanta. And Robert W. Woodruff kept it here. As Charles Seabrook, dean of science writers in the region, wrote in our newspaper, World War II was just over and "shiploads of weary soldiers, veterans of fierce battles on steamy, mosquito infested isles of the South Pacific, were coming home with battle scars of a different kind — malaria, yellow fever, encephallitis and other exotic diseases." The obscure malaria control agency in Atlanta was picked to begin training public health workers to diagnose new diseases and prevent their spread. Malaria was almost under control but polio still killed and disabled Americans by the thousands. Measles, diphtheria and tuberculosis still raged.

It was time, Washington decided, to bring the CDC home to the Potomac, but post-war Washington was cramped for space and a group of prominent Atlantans, led by Woodruff, persuaded U.S. Sen. Walter F. George to use his influence to keep the CDC in Atlanta. Woodruff provided the site, a fifteen-acre tract on Clifton road near Emory University and its hospitals. In the years that followed, the CDC has orchestrated the eradication of smallpox from the face of the earth and helped make polio, diphtheria, lockjaw and other once-common childhood killers little more than a memory in the United States.

Its scientists deal with diseases that were unheard of in the 1940's — Legionnaire's disease, toxic shock syndrome and AIDS, a deadly new disease that the CDC itself discovered. The disease which the world now knows as acquired immune deficiency syndrome came to the attention of a doctor from the CDC's elite Epidemiology Intelligence Service who learned in a casual conversation with a UCLA professor of two unusual occurrences of a rare type of pneumonia, pneumonocyustis carnii. He found three more cases, all among men under age forty who were active homosexuals. His supervisors in Atlanta told him to pursue the problem, and his report became the first word of the disease the world now knows.

It was from Atlanta that word went out a few years ago that the American Medical Association had determined that smoking was a "causative factor" in cancer.

Almost daily our science writers produce for local use, or for dispatch to professional journals, stories of some new step in the conquest of disease or some suspenseful, even exotic, research project: CDC scientists may be dispatched to investigate toxic spills in New York, illness from tainted cheese in California or an unusual death among hospitalized children in Texas. The EIS has assisted Indian health officials in the study of long-term effects of the Bhopal chemical disaster and helped Atlanta homicide experts unravel its cases of missing and murdered young blacks.

Dramatic and exciting as this era of medicine and research is, Dr. Gilbert could almost have foreseen it for his town. After all, he was a contemporary of the renowned Dr. Crawford W. Long, who pioneered in the use of anesthesia for surgery. Dr. Long's feat was performed in Jefferson, Georgia, in 1842, but he later moved to Atlanta to practice, building a home here in 1851, and today one of the bigger hospitals bears his name. (Jefferson has a museum named for him, containing relics from his practice and a diorama depicting the use of ether in his operations there.)

So swiftly did things move in Atlanta in Dr. Gilbert's day that nine years after he arrived on horseback, the community's first doctor, he saw the founding of a medical school. The Atlanta Medical College, from which Emory University School of Medicine is descended, was chartered in 1854 and was ambitiously determined to relieve southern boys of the necessity of going north to get their medical education. Things were going along well for the new medical school, but the Civil War intervened and students and faculty made haste to join the Confederate forces. (The depth of their feeling is illustrated in a story related by Miss Mildred Jordan, director of Emory's Abner Wellborn Calhoun Medical Library. On December 20, 1860, South Carolina seceded from the Union, and that night Mrs. Willis Westmoreland, wife of one of the founding doctors at Atlanta Medical College, gave birth to a daughter. They named the baby "South Carolina.")

Fans of the book and movie *Gone With the Wind* remember the scenes of terrible suffering when the wounded and dying poured into Atlanta as the fighting got closer. These scenes are well documented in history. Trainloads of the wounded came in, hospitals and public buildings overflowed and all families who could were called upon to "accommodate a wounded soldier" in their homes. The mayor issued a proclamation calling on the businessmen to close their stores at 4 P.M. so they could meet the trains and help with the wounded. All Atlanta citizens were "earnestly requested to send their carriages and their servants to assist in removing the wounded . . . by night as well as by day."

That was in the summer of 1863 when the fighting was still some distance from the city. By the spring of '64, when Sherman began his Atlanta campaign, the city was already filled to overflowing with the wounded. And still they came.

Historian Wallace P. Reed's eyewitness account of the city on the opening day of the Battle of Atlanta, July 22, is enough to make Miss Mitchell's gutsy fictional version pale. He wrote of seeing General Hood seated on his horse in a little park in front of the Kimball House and near the railroad station, receiving messages "every minute from the scene of action."

Groups of citizens, Reed explains, were gathered in the park watching the general.

"Suddenly the park was invaded by the hospital corps. Long tables were stretched out and a crowd of professional-looking men in uniform took charge of them and commenced opening their cases of instruments. They were surgeons. It was not long before ambulances and wagons rolled into the park by the dozen, and the wounded were hastily taken out and placed upon the tables. After that it was cut and slash, for the work had to be done in a hurry. The green grass took on a blood-red hue, and as the surgeon's saw crunched through the bones of the unfortunates, hundreds of gory arms and legs were thrown into the baskets prepared to receive them."

That night Mrs. Willis Westmoreland gave birth to a son. They called him "Hood."

As Sherman got closer, the wounded and dying were evacuated, and by October 7 Federal troops began their ordered destruction of the city. Wounded Federal soldiers had been brought back from the battle of Jonesboro and some of them were placed in the Atlanta Medical College. Dr. Noel D'Alvigny, a member of the faculty regarded as too old to go to war when the conflict began, found the war had come to him. He worked tirelessly caring for the wounded on both sides — service which later won for him, a French-born "Rebel," commendation from the Federal Government. Although the Federal wounded had been moved out of the Medical College by the military authorities, their presence there must have given the old doctor an idea for saving the school.

According to historian Reed, Dr. D'Alvigny called in the hospital attendants, plied them with whiskey and put them to bed with instructions to howl in pain when the military arrived. The torch squad came, but Dr. D'Alvigny stood them off. He had been in three armies, he said, but this was the first time he ever witnessed invaders so depraved as to burn a hospital filled with the wounded. The baffled Yankee officers, who thought everybody had been removed, gave Dr. D'Alvigny until daybreak to get his "patients" out.

But the next morning Sherman's army had started south "and thus, by a ruse, was the valuable building of the Atlanta Medical College saved, to be used again for the noble purpose for which it was first erected."

So the medical profession had a head start on rebuilding when the following April the war ended and people could once more consider peaceful pursuits. The Medical College had been looted of many expensive fixtures and valuable books. Dean Westmoreland's carefully tended "Garden of Medicinal Plants" was a shambles and his portrait had evidently been pierced by Minie balls. It is stored today in the Medical Library where the holes in the canvas have been repaired so the dean, observers say, appears to have a black eye.

The Atlanta Medical College not only flourished but inspired competition. Money was hard to come by during Reconstruction days and there were occasions when students, unable to pay their tuition, turned their horses over to the school to be sold. But three other medical schools were to open — Oglethorpe University's in 1870, Southern Medical College in 1887, and the Atlanta School of Medicine in 1903. One at a time they merged with each other and in 1915 became a part of growing Emory University, the little Methodist college which, heavily endowed by Coca-Cola money, today sprawls over beautiful wooded acres in Druid Hills.

The doctors running that early medical school yearned for a hospital and real patients to work on, but they were a long time coming. At one point the medical college operated at its own expense a clinic with hospital facilities and made a deal with the city to treat poor patients, either at the clinic or in their own homes, at a flat rate of fifty cents a day.

Emory's medical students today have no such problems. Its doctors work not only in the handsome Emory University Hospital, located on the campus, but in Henrietta Egleston Children's Hospital and Aidmore Hospital for Crippled Children, which are connected to Emory by underground tunnels. Crawford W. Long is a community hospital in downtown Atlanta, but Emory owns it and its doctors train there. The Veterans Administration Hospital on Clairmont Road is associated with Emory. Also near Emory Hospital is a psychiatric clinic for children, where specialists in that field train, and the State of Georgia Mental Health Institute.

But the oldest and biggest clinical teaching facility of the medical school is, of course, old Grady Hospital.

Started in 1892 in a red brick Victorian pile which looks like a residence out of the gaslight era, old Grady Hospital is in a way the heart of the city. It was named for Henry W. Grady, the editor-hero for whom so many things in Atlanta are named, but it is familiarly called "the Grady's" by indigent Atlantans to whom it has given life. A charity hospital, operated by the Fulton-DeKalb Hospital Authority and financed by taxes, Grady is where everybody, rich or poor, goes after a brush with violence — crashes, fires, poisonings, shootings or any other emergency or accidental injury.

Margaret Mitchell's husband, John Marsh, wouldn't permit an earlier arriving ambulance crew to move her the night she was struck down by a taxicab on Peachtree Street but insisted that nobody touch her until the Grady ambulance, with a doctor in attendance, arrived.

Victims of the Winecoff Hotel fire in which one hundred people were killed December 7, 1946, were taken first to Grady. I still remember the pitiful throngs of people gathered in the morgue in the basement of the old Grady, trying to identify relatives from shards of bones and poignant chunks of melted jewelry.

Nothing really reflects Atlanta's growth better than "the Grady's." Its old building thrusts out annexes in all directions and underground corridors to connect with equally ramshackle units across the street. It was crowded, hopelessly dingy and a melange of the worse smells of illness, disinfectant and poverty.

On sunny days visitors filled the benches on the sidewalk, listening sometimes with a mystification to Grady's famous "talking magnolia tree." A speaker from the hospital public address system hung from a branch, well-hidden by foliage, and it was strange and a little fearsome, unless you knew about it, to hear a voice emanating from the tree shrilly paging doctors, who might be crossing the street between buildings.

"Saturday night at the Grady" has always been high drama. Victims from wrecks and shooting matches and cutting scrapes and drinking sprees are hauled into the emergency clinic, along with old people, taken mysteriously ill in the night, and feverish, fretful babies come down with urgent rashes and croups.

The talking magnolia tree still stands and still speaks and Saturday nights in the emergency clinic are pretty much the same. When it was built in 1958, Grady Hospital's building was one of the handsomest things on the skyline — a tall clean rectangle of a building which cost $25 million and which gleamingly housed more than a thousand patients (not counting 325 bassinets for new arrivals) and treated half a million out-patients each year. With nearly thirty years' age on it, the old hospital has grown shabby and terribly overcrowded and in 1986 its administrator, Bill Pinkston, was looking forward to a bond issue to finance a remodelling program which would cost between $100 million and $150 million. The out-patient load has grown to 800,000 because of the hospital's poison and burn units and its high risk infant and maternity care facilities.

Its eighth floor, as warmly and invitingly furnished as a college fraternity house, operates as a psychiatric intensive treatment center, run in conjunction with the State Health Department and Emory.

The current hospital will stand, augmented by a new building to house clinics across the street, but the heartening thing to Atlantans, who love it, is that the old original "Grady's" red brick mansion will also survive as a hospital office building.

Although medical training in Atlanta is centered in Emory and the school accounts for about half of the $10 million spent annually in almost five hundred projects here, there are many other hospitals and groups engaging in research. Morehouse College, part of the big Atlanta University complex, founded for the education of blacks and now biracial, graduated its first class of young doctors from its medical school in the spring of 1986.

Dr. Gilbert, riding into town with his whistle and his quinine more than a century ago, was the beginning of it all.

Atlanta Newspapers — A Prejudiced View

CHAPTER XI

They say the wife is always the last to know, and I never understood better how she, poor wretch, must feel than I did in the spring of 1950. I was practically the last to know about the merger of the two big Atlanta newspapers.

Just as the deceived wife, who finds that her husband is involved with another, must start mentally retracing the path, trying to remember where her attention was when he started these shenanigans, I think back to the merger as somehow coming about because I was bogged down in that elephant idiocy.

It doesn't matter now, of course. The thing is past. The morning *Atlanta Constitution*, founded in 1868 and published by the Howell family since 1876, and the evening *Atlanta Journal*, founded in 1883 and published by the Cox family of Ohio since 1939, are under one roof and one ownership now. If it was not a love match but a marriage of convenience with, editorially speaking, separate beds and separate rooms for the partners, it's still a lot different from the way things were the winter an old elephant named Alice died at the Atlanta City Zoo.

The two newspapers lived apart and were as hotly competitive as is possible with different deadlines and different press times. We of the *Constitution* staff had only recently moved into a new building at the corner of Forsyth and Alabama Streets (later acquired by the Georgia Power company but vacant and boarded up in 1986) and were feeling smug, albeit a little homesick for the dingy, cupolated old Victorian home across the street where Henry Grady, Joel Chandler Harris and Frank L. Stanton had worked. The *Journal* also had new digs — a whole refurbished office building and, going up cheek by jowl, a new structure to house its mechanical departments.

There was outwardly nothing to indicate we were about to be blended.

And then, as I said, that old elephant named Alice died. I was out of town covering a murder trial at the time and paid scant attention to the emotional stories in both papers about this cataclysmic tragedy at the zoo and the widespread mourning among kiddies. The jury brought in an acquittal for the defendant in my murder trial (a state senator) and I came home to pick up a new assignment.

"This is right down your alley," said Luke Greene, our then city editor — and I winced, recognizing the preface to a clinker of a chore.

It was.

"I want you to get us an elephant for the zoo," said Mr. Greene. "You may have noticed the *Journal* has started a campaign for one. So you'll have to get us a bigger and better elephant — and get it faster."

I had indeed noticed that the *Journal* had a campaign going to buy a replacement for Alice. How could I miss with my own children, sharper than a serpent's tooth, demanding dimes to contribute to it through their school? The *Journal*'s elephant drive was surging ahead, no school child left unturned.

For a day or two I followed the same tack, working children's hospitals and orphanages and coming up with a grand total of $7.82. After about a week I knew I had to find an angle for our elephant campaign, and I started casting about for some public-spirited citizen in whose heart there burned — or could be kindled

— philanthropy and a tender regard for elephants.

It came to me in the middle of the night: Asa Griggs Candler, Jr.

Mr. Candler, son of the founder of the Coca-Cola Company, was a man who thought so highly of elephants he once maintained a stable of them in the front yard of his home on Briarcliff Road. In fact, he may have been the only man on the continent of North America to plow his kitchen garden with elephants. He had a whole zoo on his grounds, established after his first wife had, on a trip west, expressed a desire to have an antelope for a pet. She found one waiting for her when she got home, the nucleus of a full-scale zoo.

The neighbors complained about every aspect of that zoo, smells, sounds and escapes. Some people had even gone to court about it, among them one badly shaken woman who went out to get in her car one morning and found a fugitive monkey behind the steering wheel. Mr. Candler had reluctantly given up his menagerie, presenting the whole works to the city, including four elephants — the forerunners of the late lamented Alice. Their names: Coca, Cola, Pause and Refreshes.

I didn't know Mr. Candler, but I was desperate. I put in a call to his public relations expert, a nice young man named Harold Brown. Would Mr. Candler, proven friend of the zoo, care to go for another elephant?

Harold wasn't sure that Mr. Candler would feel like further philanthropy in this direction. Atlanta's zoo was then terribly run down and seedy-looking. His other pachyderm gifts there had not flourished. Pause, Refreshes and Coca had preceded Alice in death. Even multimillionaires aren't eager to throw good elephants after bad.

However, Harold promised to talk to Mr. Candler and call me back. I moped around the office, scrounging a few elephant fund coins where I could — and thinking about Mr. Candler. His public relations, even to my untutored eye, looked a bit frayed and in need of mending. The zoo suits had been followed by a fire in his dry-cleaning establishment, in which hundreds of Atlanta citizens had literally lost the shirts off their backs. And before that could be adjusted, Mr. Candler had embarked on a program to take the tombstones out of old Westview cemetery, which he owned, and make it a modern, park-like burying place with vast sweeps of green lawn, all perpetually cuttable by power mower. The howls of outraged citizens were even then reverberating throughout the Fulton County courthouse.

Harold Brown called me back. Mr. Candler would see me — in his office in a vast, windowless building in the middle of Westview Cemetery.

Well, the result of our meeting was, from my point of view, fantastically successful. Mr. Candler, who in his youth had been an African big game hunter in the best Hemingway tradition, would on the following Saturday give a wild animal party for children in his trophy room in the cemetery. At the height of the party he would unveil a check made payable "To the Children of Atlanta" in the amount of whatever sum would be needed to supplement the lagging *Constitution* elephant fund. In exchange we were to conduct an essay contest, "Why I Would Like to Help Select Coca II," with six school children winners to fly with Mr. Candler in his private plane into the wilds of darkest New Hampshire to Benson's Wild Animal Farm.

There were minor disparagements. On the very Sunday the *Constitution* triumphantly bannered this story with a picture of Mr. Candler, children and check on the front page, columnist Doris Lockerman, who had not been apprised of the coup, wrote on an inside page that there were plenty of rich men in Atlanta who could buy an elephant for the zoo but that we didn't want that — "We want the elephant to be bought with the pennies of children." And at Sunday School one of my dearest friends remarked churlishly that *that* Asa Candler had committed the crowning outrage of his career — "wild animal party on the hallowed ground of old Westview."

But I weathered them and the most wholesale-entered essay contest I ever saw, and early one spring day photographer Marion Johnson and I met Mr. Candler, his press agent Harold Brown, his son-in-law Tom Callaway, City Parks Director George Simon and six essay winners at the airport to take off for New Hampshire.

Our departure was only slightly clouded by a brief story in the morning paper to the effect that during the night the *Journal* had attended the going-out-of-business sale of a defunct circus in

Athens and brought home, under cover of darkness, a moth-eaten little old elephant, to be named "Penny" — for guess whose pennies?

Beating them to their own announcement had taken the zing out of their story, we felt, even if the razzle-dazzle of our elephant hunt had not. And it was a razzle-dazzle hunt, for sure. Mr. Candler was an aviation enthusiast. His harness race track was the site of the Atlanta Airport and he was one of the first businessmen in America to acquire a private plane. So he had a luxury, twenty-passenger plane with two pilots to take us first to Washington, where we were received by his old college roommate, the Veep, Vice-President Alben Barkley. We had a day of sight-seeing by chartered bus and then on to Boston, where another chartered bus picked us up for the trip to New Hampshire and the wild-animal farm.

The essay winners picked an elephant, with only a little prompting from Mr. Candler and me. (He knew quality and I was interested in size.) We flew back to Atlanta and the elephant, dispatched with bands playing and flags flying and a ceremony attended by the mayor of the town, was to follow us in a heated van with a vet in attendance.

He was due on Saturday, and on Thursday our then managing editor, Lee Rogers (now assistant to the president at Lockheed) flung another journalistic hand grenade in my direction.

"We should have a parade to welcome our elephant," he said. "Get one up."

It would have been a little silly to protest that I was a reporter and not a promoter since I had already promoted an elephant. So numbly, not knowing the first thing about it, I set to work and by Friday night I had conned every acquaintance, every new source at my command into putting something — bands, clowns, tumblers, *anything* — into the parade. As an afterthought I looked around for a parade marshall, and Mike Benton, longtime Southeastern Fair impresario and a veteran of many parades, came to my rescue. It was he who mentioned the matter of the police permit.

Police Chief Herbert Jenkins, normally a brave man, blanched in horror.

"Do you realize it's Easter Saturday?" he whispered. "We can't add a parade to that traffic!"

Eventually, of course, the chief relented. And after a bad night, during which I alternately tossed fitfully and phoned the State Patrol to be sure the *Journal* had not hijacked our elephant, we were ready for the arrival of Coca II.

Gov. Herman Talmadge was not available for official welcoming but Mayor Hartsfield was, and the First Lady and the little Talmadge sons, Bobby and Gene, were going to meet Coca II in front of the *Constitution* building and give him his "first taste of Georgia peanuts."

The *Journal*'s then city editor Bob Collins declined our telegraphed invitation to cover the festivities, but everybody else was there, radio, television, wire services and newsreel.

Our chief, Ralph McGill, emceed the show from the *Constitution* lobby — in front of the gold seal which reads, "Wisdom, Justice, Moderation." At the crucial moment, when we hoped the eyes of the world were riveted on our triumph, the little Talmadge boys, their hands loaded with Georgia peanuts, took one look at Coca II and turned tail and ran, howling in terror.

Editor McGill snatched up Gene, the eldest — named for his grandfather, the old governor — spanked him soundly and thrust him back to do his duty.

Beautiful Betty Talmadge was mighty gracious about it when Mr. McGill apologized to her afterward. He didn't know what possessed him to start spanking the child, he confessed ruefully, unless it was reflex action — the old irresistible urge to hit a Talmadge.

I slunk home for a week's vacation. And the very next Saturday our political editor at the time, the late M.L. St. John, telephoned me to tell me that the Sunday papers were to announce the merger of the *Constitution* with the *Journal*.

"We might not need you any more," he warned me. "We've decided to put all our elephants in one basket."

Time magazine recorded the event another way: "Atlanta now has two newspapers, two elephants and one publisher."

When I began this chapter on Atlanta newspapers, friends tactfully suggested that I might have trouble combating a bit of natural bias. After all, a newspaper woman who thinks journalism is a holy cause and the *Atlanta Constitution* practically its anointed apostle, how could I be sure of giving an objective picture of the field? Was it possible for me to render an impartial judgment between my own *Constitution*, for instance, and those people downstairs on the *Journal*?

Certainly it's possible. I can leave all personal feeling out of this and do a careful, accurate job of factual reporting. In fact, I did — for fifteen of the dullest pages I ever read in my life. I have thrown them in the trash basket. Anybody who wants a good careful, accurate job of factual reporting on this subject could have gotten James Reston or Theodore White. Or, maybe easier, telephone the newspapers' promotion department and request the vital statistics in easy, mimeographed capsule form.

When you get an insider's view, you get feeling — love, loyalty, prejudice, antagonism and maybe a corny kind of special family humor.

So I begin with prejudice.

The *Constitution* is my paper. It's famous, faulty, full of courage and utterly individual. I would have died if I hadn't got a job on it, because even down in South Alabama, where its circulation was, at most, spotty, I was reared to believe that the *Constitution* was the South's greatest newspaper and one of the world's most distinguished, a belief not dispelled even now.

The *Journal* is a good newspaper, lively, aggressive, well written, well edited and at the time of the merger it had more circulation than the *Constitution* — an edge the *Constitution* has since reclaimed. In the classic words of the prejudiced everywhere, some of my best friends are *Journal* people. This isn't a local situation, of course. Newspaper people always gravitate to other newspaper people, setting aside their professional rivalry after hours to enjoy their common interests. But it may be especially true in Atlanta because so many people have worked on both staffs.

Of course, back in 1950 the *Journal* staff was as apprehensive about the merger as we were. Politicians shouted, "Monopoly!" Advertisers expected the worst, although there were about twenty other papers, one daily, the *Marietta Journal*, and the others weeklies in the Atlanta area at that time. (In 1986 there were eight dailies and thirty-seven weeklies.) Reporters and editors on both sides of the viaduct were certain some of us wouldn't, as Saint said, "be needed any more."

Many people at the *Journal* had gone through a similar experience in 1939. The day of the "Gone With the Wind" premiere, with the whole town in carnival mood, they had learned that the *Journal* and its radio station, WSB, had been sold, and so had the other afternoon paper, William Randolph Hearst's *Atlanta Georgian*. The buyer was the head of the Cox chain, James M. Cox, the colorful former governor of Ohio, who with Franklin D. Roosevelt as his teammate had run against Warren G. Harding for president in 1920.

The *Journal* had fared fine under the new ownership, but the *Georgian* had folded and its editors and reporters scattered. Some, of course, found a berth on the *Journal*, some on the *Constitution*, but many had to move on to other cities or quit the newspaper business altogether.

Nobody at the *Constitution*, except possibly one or two in the highest echelon, had ever dreamed that Major Clark Howell, whose father and grandfather had preceded him at the helm, would ever relinquish the famous old paper. To sell out was crushing enough, but this was selling out to the enemy. We felt certain we would be gobbled up, absorbed, lose our identity completely. We heard all kinds of sinister things about the way they ran the *Journal*.

We heard it was one of those efficient, clean-desk operations. They were understood to pay reporters more, but they were picky about hours and expense accounts. On the *Constitution* before we moved into our new building, we had to share desks and sometimes wait in line for a typewriter. And there was a *Constitution* reporter of legend who had kept a U-Drive-It and had drawn expense money for weeks on a voucher which said succinctly: "Covering floods in Alabama." I don't know when, if ever, the bookkeeping department learned that this was during a season of prolonged drought in our neighboring state.

The *Journal* rode buses on assignment. We grandly took taxis, signing the meter tickets. You had to have a pass to get in the *Journal* building at night. The *Constitution* stairway was a sort of ascending flophouse for old newsies and visiting bums and drunks who slept there out of the cold in winter. (A subscriber once complained to Major Howell that he found a bedbug in his morning paper and the major is said to have replied cheerfully, "What do you expect for a nickel?")

Taking whiskey into the *Journal* building was a firing offense. To old hands on the *Constitution*, a few drinks and a game of poker around the copy desk after the paper was put to bed came under the head of wholesome employee recreation. The *Journal* was said to have a splendid well-run reference department with complete clip files and a professional librarian in charge. The *Constitution* had a file room, presided over part time by a kid who was going to Tech, and when you were looking for a picture or a clipping, you sometimes blundered into a filing cabinet of empty liquor bottles and old sandwich crusts.

The *Journal* had a Sunday supplement, precisely and exquisitely produced for more than forty years under the direction of Angus Perkerson. Our Sunday supplement consisted of a couple of feature pages put together by a brilliant, erratic old Hearst man who bragged that he had been fired from nearly every paper in the country, "but never for incompetence, always for drinking."

The *Constitution's* business operation was something out of a Dickens novel, a sleeve garter and alpaca vest thing run by a kindly old gentleman who mended his glasses with twine, devoted his lunch hours to playing pinochle down at the fire station and, as awed observers later noted, "spent a dollar to save a dime any day." The *Constitution's* circulation department was run by a union so exclusive it was easier for a newcomer to town to get in the Piedmont Driving Club than to get a subscription to the paper.

What then, you may wonder, did the *Constitution* have to bring to this merger?

It had history and a tradition of service. Born in crisis and named in optimism, it was founded in 1868 when carpetbag rule harassed Georgia. The paper's name was suggested by President Andrew Johnson as appropriate for a newspaper seeking to restore constitutional government to the South.

It had color. It drew characters. Being in that newsroom was so much fun staff members hung around on their own time — no time-and-a-half overtime consideration. I remember one night during the war a young soldier and his girl wandered in asking how they could get married in a hurry before he was shipped overseas.

They were strangers in town and had practically no money. We didn't have any money either but we had connections. We whipped them up a newsroom wedding in nothing flat. The late city recorder Luke Arnold was rounded up to officiate, the famous Negro accordionist, Graham Jackson, troubadour to President Franklin D. Roosevelt, was recruited to play the wedding march. The city editor gave the bride away, the copy desk served as groomsmen, the church editor as maid of honor. We took up a collection and hired them a hotel room for their honeymoon and then, full of sentiment and file room punch, we danced dreamily to accordion music.

Schoolchildren tours still come to Atlanta newspapers, sedately conducted by young women from the promotion department. But the *Constitution* of the old days used to give them a real show. When we heard them coming, the boys used to scramble for hats to set on the back of their heads, stick press cards in the bands and rend the air with cries of "Flash!" and "Stop the press!" And pint-sized Lee Fuhrman, then city editor, was never too busy to respond royally, "Get me Joe Stalin on the phone! Get me Eleanor Roosevelt!"

Writers and reporters, photographers and artists seem to have flourished in this easy, unregimented atmosphere. Four times the *Constitution* has won Pulitzer prizes — once in 1931 for Herman Hancock's reporting of city hall graft, in 1958 for Ralph McGill's editorials, in 1959 for Jack Nelson's expose of conditions at the state mental hospital and in 1966 for Eugene Patterson's general editorial excellence but specifically for his defense of the right of a young black named Julian Bond to be seated in the Georgia House of Representatives. (The *Journal*'s single Pulitzer award went to a reporter named George Goodwin in 1949 for his stories about tomb-stone voting in old Gene Talmadge's last race for governor.)

Looking back, it's funny that in 1950 we of the *Constitution* didn't dream that the new owners really knew or valued the odd, obstreperous, perversely accomplished crew at the *Constitution*. Merger, we said, ha. More likely a submerger.

Two people were soon to learn better.

Ralph McGill, the stocky, perpetually worried-looking man who had risen from the ranks as a sportswriter to become one of the country's more famous editors, and his next in command, Jack Tarver, were summoned to Miami to talk with Governor Cox. They came away awestruck.

The old gentleman knew a great deal about the operation of both papers, including the names and comparative talents of minor editors and writers. He wanted the combined Sunday paper to be a blending of the best of each. He asked Tarver to take a hand in directing the operation. As for McGill, he was a long-time McGill fan, and he had but one order for him — the only one, Mr. McGill said, the old governor gave him from that day until his death at the age of eighty-seven in 1957. He wanted the McGill column to be moved from the editorial page to column one, page one.

For Jack Tarver, thirty-three years old and just home from a year spent in South America on a Fulbright fellowship, the merger meant new direction to a career with which he was getting restless and dissatisfied. It meant use for hitherto unused talents. Tarver was to drop the highly successful editorial page column which he wrote for the *Constitution* and join George C. Biggers, president of the new combine, in the task of management.

Some readers were unreconciled to the change, remembering with a feeling of real loss the lethally amusing Tarverisms. A brief column, seldom running more than half a dozen paragraphs, it commented on the political and social scene with such humor that, as one victim pointed out, "You die laughing before you even notice you've been fatally harpooned."

Tarver made the change, not only cheerfully but with a sense of larger destiny, looking on it as an opportunity, among other things, to free the *Constitution* from business problems which had bedeviled its old-fashioned management and to bolster its editorial independence.

"Somebody has to steady the soapbox," he remarked with characteristic irreverence.

Jack had an answer for all the erstwhile fellow toilers in the dirty, crowded old *Constitution* newsroom when they marveled that the moon-faced, bespectacled young man who used to hunch over his typewriter, agonizingly sweating out humor in a cubbyhole back of the elevator, knew how to run this mammoth enterprise.

"Hell, I ran a country weekly, didn't I?" he asked, recalling his first job in Lyons, Georgia, (now center of the Vidalia onion country) and poking a crooked forefinger at you by way of illustration. "I bet I'm the only metropolitan publisher in the country who ever caught a hand in a flatbed press."

The name of Ralph McGill was, of course, synonymous with that of the *Constitution*. There are places in the world, mostly those accessible only by camelback, where Atlanta, even America, was known chiefly because it was the home of the *Constitutions*'s McGill. Sometimes he was referred to as the conscience of the South, and in Atlanta his function was frequently summed up in the words of one subscriber who said simply, "He does my thinking for me."

Death eventually rewrote the masthead of our paper. Mr. McGill died February 3, 1961, and friends and admirers flocked into Atlanta from all over the world to pay tribute at his funeral, including such varied celebrities as Vice President Hubert Humphrey and lovelorn columnist Ann Landers. Gene Patterson succeeded him as editor (McGill was publisher at the time of his death) and some of us felt that our days of news-making, as well as news reporting, were over. Mr. McGill, coming out for fair treatment of blacks long before "integration" was more than a crossword puzzle type word, had brought down on himself the wrath of the Ku Klux Klan with robed men and assorted other dissenters picketing our building regularly. Bomb threats and poison pen letters came almost daily and so, of course, did representatives of the other side — admiring newsmen, television crews and such notables as John and Robert Kennedy. (When he was president, John Kennedy chose the *Constitution* as one of a half dozen newspapers he read daily, which pleased Mr. McGill enormously. Tarver was less enchanted because of the high cost of getting the paper to the airport, on a plane to Washington and delivered to the White House in time for the President's breakfast. When he grumbled, half jokingly, Mr. McGill offered to pay the tab himself which, of course, Tarver wouldn't allow.)

Even as we lamented the passing of our day in the national spotlight, a young man was coming to join us little knowing that he would hurtle us into the nation's news for quite a spell. He was Reg Murphy, our one-time political editor, who went away for a few years to do something improbably called management consultant. When Gene Patterson left us to go to the *Washington Post* and later to the *St. Petersburg Times* as publisher, Reg returned to the paper as editor.

All of us who worked with Reg liked him, and except for one strange act, we paid him no more attention than reporters normally pay editors. The strange act was that for the first time in its illustrious history he had the *Constitution* come out editorially for a Republican — embarrassingly enough, Richard Nixon! Startling as this was, it, too, passed and had been, we hoped, lived down when one February night in 1974 Jim Minter, managing editor, answered his phone to hear these words: "This is Reg Murphy. I've been kidnapped by the American Revolutionary Army."

Minter had come up from a job in the sports department and was probably preparing a snappy comeback when a second and strange voice said, "We'll be in touch with you in another way."

He knew then it was no laughing matter. Reg *had* been kidnapped.

The staff spun into action. A kidnapping was something to cover and this was *our* kidnapping. I went out to Reg's house to be with his family and the FBI agents stationed there. Other reporters were deployed at police headquarters and any other place where some break might come. William H. Fields, executive editor of both papers, set up a press room to accommodate news, radio and television reporters who were pouring in from all parts of the world. On the FBI's suggestion that he might be the next victim, Hal Gulliver, associate editor, accepted special security arrangements.

For two days and two nights Reg was bound, gagged and blindfolded, imprisoned first, he felt, in a motel and then in a residence.

His captor was a man who called himself "the Colonel." He had telephoned Reg with a story about owning his own construction company and having 300,000 gallons of fuel oil, badly needed by every charitable institution in town, which he would give away if Reg would meet with him. He arrived at Reg's house about supper time and asked Reg to accompany him in his car. They were barely out of sight when he said formally, "Mr. Murphy, you have been kidnapped.

We're going to stop these lying, leftist, liberal news media!"

The next word at the paper was that the kidnappers had called with a demand for $700,000 ransom money.

There was no question about shelling out the money. Jack Tarver didn't even take time to check with the Cox family, owners of the paper. He called the Federal Reserve bank, the paper's next-door neighbors on Marietta Street, and like any good neighbor bringing over a cup of sugar, bank officials arrived at the back door with a sack full of currency.

The only question was if Reg was alive. How could we be sure?

It must have seemed a reasonable question to the kidnapper. He let Reg call his secretary, Mrs. Mary Murphy (no relation) with a message she could identify as definitely from Reg. When he quoted some favorite lines from William Faulkner's Nobel prize acceptance speech, she was certain.

"I believe that man will not merely endure, he will prevail," said Reg, and Mary, tears in her eyes, nodded her head. Reg was alive.

The next question was how to deliver the ransom. The kidnapper was specific. Although it was a bitter cold day, he insisted that it be delivered by a hatless, coatless man, wearing a white short-sleeved shirt and tennis shoes and driving an open Jeep. The spot picked was a highway sign on Georgia 400 about twenty-five miles from the newspaper office.

Jim Minter took the assignment himself.

Jim was a *Journal* alumnus, lately come to the *Constitution* and not nearly as close to Reg as those of us who had worked with him all along. When he put on that white summery shirt and the tennis shoes, picked up the sack containing $700,000 and headed for the dark, cold alley where a borrowed Jeep was parked, those of us watching choked up. It was, we all knew, a dangerous mission. It could have ended with his being kidnapped too or even killed. I remembered a classic McGillism. All managing editors, he liked to say, are of necessity sons of bitches. If so, Jim Minter was *our* son of a bitch. We loved him.

Minter delivered the money and notified the FBI. The kidnapper delivered Reg to a parking lot outside a motel in neighboring DeKalb county.

The kidnapper, a man named William A. H. Williams, was quickly arrested and the ransom money was recovered and returned to the kind neighbor who lent it. Williams was found guilty on three charges of kidnapping and sentenced to serve forty years in prison. His wife, Betty Ruth, pleaded guilty to concealing a felony and received a three-year suspended sentence.

Reg was to leave us to take a job as publisher of the *San Francisco Herald Examiner*, owned by the William Randolph Hearst family who themselves knew something about kidnapping from the experience of their daughter, Patty. Later Reg became publisher of the *Baltimore Sun*. Both Tarver and Bill Fields retired. And Minter moved up to the post of editor of both papers.

Two new jobs, editorial page editor, were created. Durwood McAllister, who had served the *Journal* in half a dozen capacities after a stint at the *Birmingham Age-Herald* and the *Anniston Star*, became the chief of their editorial department. Tom Teepen joined the *Constitution* as editorial page editor after fourteen years in that post with the *Dayton Daily News*.

The news and feature staffs of both papers were blended, a cable television station came aboard and the papers began reaching out into the neighboring counties with weekly "extras" aimed at covering their particular news. Seven of these bureaus flourish in the suburban areas and the inner city.

Just as the papers cover the homely happenings in the little towns and few remaining rural areas around Atlanta, they have acquired, through the Cox hookup, reporters in all the major capitals of the world, feature and news sharing with twenty-one other Cox newspapers. This in addition to the lively staff assigned to the Washington bureau.

Before his death, Ralph McGill sometimes wondered wryly what an editor does when all the old battles are won. Apparently old battles are always succeeded by new ones. Gene Patterson saw the papers' challenge as education and industrial development. Tom Teepen and Durwood McAllister don't consider that those problems have gone away. They have been augmented by others — technological education, McAllister emphasizes, and what Teepen calls "a little more of a knack for bi-racialism" and the "will, the nerve, the insight to build human structures which could be a model to the nation and the world."

Minter regards Atlanta newspapers as particularly lucky in their location in a capital city — almost unique among big city papers — placing them in the heart of the state and the region. Covering business news has become a major concern of the newspapers, enlisting the talents of a big staff and filling entire sections of newsprint. Now, says Minter, the quality of life in Atlanta calls for increased attention to the arts for the growing sophistication of our readership.

Well, Mr. Asa Candler is dead now, and his home where Atlanta elephants got their start is now a state hospital, dealing largely with alcoholism — a poetic use of an estate that soft drink built. There's a whole new zoo at Grant Park, including a new elephant house. I haven't checked on Coca II in years, but then I've been busy and it's possible she had nothing to do with the destiny of Atlanta newspapers after all.

"Ain't That a Van Gogh?"

CHAPTER XII

When Chief Justice Earl Warren of the U.S. Supreme Court came to Atlanta to make a speech at Georgia Tech in 1963, there was a minor movement among members of the local John Birch Society to make him feel unwelcome. Signs saying "Impeach Earl Warren" were hoisted in a few places and there were threats of an airport demonstration to express displeasure at his desegregation decision.

Mayor Ivan Allen, unwilling to have such a prominent guest go away with the feeling that our town was inhospitable, promptly alerted the police force and then he himself met Mr. Justice Warren's plane and cordially but stubbornly stuck to him closer than a brother for the duration of his visit.

When the visit ended without incident, the *New York Times'* local man then, Claude Sitton, asked a police official if safeguarding the chief justice had been much of a job.

"Oh, hell no," the officer said easily. "We got more men on Whistler's Mother than we had on him!"

Whatever the Police Department's reasoning, the emphasis was exactly right. The preponderance of Atlanta's population was a great deal more interested in art than it was in a grudge session with Chief Justice Earl Warren.

In fact, even at that moment throngs which were in a few weeks to total more than 118,000 people were filing through the Atlanta Art Association's McBurney Hall to take a look at James McNeill Whistler's maternal parent and a French traveling companion, "The Penitent St. Mary Magdalene" by Georges de la Tour, who had arrived in Atlanta from the Louvre a couple of days before the Chief Justice.

The presence of these two famous paintings in Atlanta's then unpretentious, unspectacular museum was, in a way, evidence that the city was, as one artist happily phrased it, "ripping into a cultural renaissance that won't wait."

They were on loan from the French government in tribute to 122 Atlantans who were killed in a jetliner which crashed and burned on takeoff from Orly Airport in France the morning of June 3, 1962. These people, leaders in Atlanta's social, civic and artistic life, were homeward bound after touring European art centers on a trip sponsored by the Atlanta Art Association. The crash was a disaster and a stunning blow to our town, where there were few people who did not have ties of friendship, kinship or business with one or more of the victims.

For months there were recurring reminders of the tragedy.

Mayor Allen went to Paris to investigate the crash and to make arrangements for the return of the few sad remnants of the bodies and the belongings of the people who had been on the holiday. There were memorial services as bodies were identified and brought home and then the wrenching practical concerns — auctions of homes and furnishings of couples on the plane, an embarrassed inquiry from a vet about what to do with the pets he had been boarding for several of the travelers, a notice in the personal column on the society page that a family of children, orphaned by the crash, were moving away to live with relatives.

The French ambassador in Washington, His Excellency, Herve Alphand, announced that his government wished to send pictures from the Louvre — a token of friendship by which "France expresses her sympathy toward a city whose artistic and intellectual elite suffered severe losses in a plane accident at Orly."

Out of the grief and loss, however, Atlanta, which years ago took the phoenix bird of mythology as her symbol, found a way to build once more on disaster. It decided to build a new and bigger art school as a memorial to those who died.

A campaign was immediately launched to "create a living, working, producing and teaching memorial to the memory of these members . . . a new Atlanta School of Art."

Atlanta has had an art school and a museum since 1927, housed at first in the old home of Mrs. J.M. High, whose family department store once flourished on Whitehall Street. They grew to take in neighboring homes on both sides, and the school, swelled by veterans after World War II, spread to barracks-like temporary buildings in the backyard. It now occupies space in the Woodruff Arts Center, the South's largest arts consortium, raised with $20 million from individual and corporate donors and $2.5 million raised for general support in unprecedented simultaneous fund drives in 1985.

Helen Smith, who writes of things cultural for our newspapers, observed early in 1986 that Atlanta "now stands on the threshold of national and even international prominence" in the way of arts. "Whether it crosses that threshold and becomes indeed the cultural capital of the South is still a matter of conjecture. But the climate has changed in metropolitan Atlanta. As highways and high rises multiply like rabbits, so, too, are the arts increasing their birth and survival rate."

The signs, she felt, were plain to see: the new High Museum "in all its dramatic whiteness" standing like a beacon on Peachtree Street, a satellite High opening in downtown in the Georgia Pacific headquarters; the Paris concerts of the Atlanta Symphony orchestra and chorus, directed by the famed Robert Shaw, the largest ensemble of American musicians ever to go abroad; the resurgence of the Atlanta Ballet, the rejuvenated Atlanta Opera Company and an almost unbelievable flurry of excitement in the theatre.

There is without a doubt a new public awareness of the arts. The Fulton County Arts Council, created in 1979, poured $1.4 million into arts in the last year, part of the money going for important research projects such as Artsplan 2000, an extensive look at the status, needs and goals of the local arts groups. This included a feasibility study to determine if Atlanta is ready for and capable of

The dazzling High Museum of Art, designed by Richard Meier

a major national festival of black arts before the end of the decade. The state of Georgia began to take an interest a decade ago, establishing arts support groups in the state. In 1985 it made grants totalling $1.7 million to 266 arts organizations throughout the state.

The museum building itself is notable. Designed by Richard Meier, it has won several prestigious awards, drawing architectural and art writers from around the nation and abroad when it was opened — "the most visible sign," Mrs. Smith wrote, "that dramatic things are happening in the arts in Atlanta. The city's theatres, ballet and symphony have not been sleeping." The light and airy building has room for important traveling exhibits such as "China: 7000 Years of Discovery," "Dutch Masterpieces of the Golden Age," and "Wealth of the Ancient World," all major shows which couldn't have been accommodated a few years ago.

There are more than two dozen active theatre groups, three of which have sent plays by local playwrights to Broadway. There is a Center for Puppetry Arts and a new Museum of Art and Archaeology at Emory University. Touring companies of major Broadway shows book in regularly at the Fox Theatre, the mammoth Moroccan movie palace which was slated for the wrecker's ball a few years ago but saved by an uprising of devoted citizens. (Everywhere you went you saw "Save the Fox" signs on bumpers and billboards, leading one Atlanta visitor to suppose that the locals were trying to wipe out fox-hunting.)

And to think that twenty years ago a flippant fellow with paint on his hands told me art was the exclusive province of "old ladies with old money."

A fine zeal for pictures and sculpture and even doodads made of rope and beads propelled Atlanta to go thousands strong to Piedmont Park every spring for the big ten-day Piedmont Arts Festival. This whingding, launched in 1954 by a group of Buckhead artists, became an artistic free-for-all where everybody's endeavors were warmly welcomed, always admired and usually sold. Carolyn Becknell Mann, one of the founders, said the rule at first was come-one-come-all. Nothing was banned "except number paintings and real nude nudes."

The standards are stiffer now. The festival has been moved to the fall but the crowds still come in bluejeans and shorts, pushing strollers, pulling flotillas of small children and munching hotdogs as they look. Some of the most appreciative art patrons are children who have been through the public schools' art sessions wherein pictures have gone out into the rural areas with the bookmobiles.

Miss Emily Rose Wood, who directed the original program, knew that it was on target when a barefoot, overall-clad first grader watched the librarian unload prints at a country school and finally spoke up.

"Ain't that a Van Gogh?" he asked.

"His knowledge of grammar might have been shakey," the librarian said, "but his knowledge of art was right on the button."

Taking art to the rural reaches of the county was important when there were more rural reaches to be found around Atlanta. Now that subdivisions are gobbling up all the old farmlands and corn fields are sprouting office complexes and condominiums, Atlanta is more and more turning its attention to culture for the inner city dwellers and those people who make the daily trek to town on the sleek and fast little trains of the MARTA (Metropolitan Atlanta

Rapid Transit Authority) system. Of twenty-nine of MARTA's stations, twenty-two have been embellished with murals and sculpture. These range from gauzy clouds and bucolic farm scenes at one station to what-you-may-call-it contrivances of aluminum or lead in some others. After spending nearly a million dollars to ornament the stations, the MARTA board of directors turned frugal and stopped buying art, but most weary travelers, resting their eyes on the stations' walls, figure they'll get back to it when the big system is complete.

Curtis Patterson, whose sculptures adorn the Lenox MARTA station and Hartsfield International Airport, finds Atlantans receptive to the embellishment and tolerant beyond the people in such cities as New York, where there are strident protests and even lawsuits over art found to be unpleasing.

The written word is both an artistic endeavor and an industry in Atlanta, a cultural achievement and a cult. Since "that little Mitchell girl" achieved such phenomenal success, everybody who could scratch up a few Blue Horse tablets and pencil lead to apply thereon bombarded New York editors and publishers with their prose. Those who were not bold enough to send off their works stowed them away in bureau drawers against the time when some hopeful young editor, dreaming of another GWTW, came to town on a manuscript foraging expedition.

That has changed remarkably in the last few years since a soft-spoken woman named Helen Elliott, who had published some music, decided to try her hand at publishing books. As her son, Wayne Elliott, now president of the company, says affectionately, "She never knew any better."

Happily, Mrs. Elliott didn't have to learn any better. Her little enterprise, called Peachtree Publishers, Ltd., was a success from the start. Her first book, a charmingly illustrated fantasy called, *If I Found a Wistful Unicorn,* was an instant hit. Writers who had had no luck with the big trade publishers in New York and Boston began lugging their manuscripts to Mrs. Elliott. She read everything with a warm and natural sympathy for the writer and a sharp eye on the manuscript's commercial potential.

Lewis Grizzard, humor columnist for the Atlanta newspaper,

put together a collection of his pieces and called them, *Kathy Sue Loudermilk, I Love You.*

Both the author and the publisher had it made. Grizzard suddenly became the hottest thing on the literary scene, turning out more and more books, some of which hit the *New York Times* bestseller list and all of which caught the eye of paperback publishers. Peachtree's next coup came from a smalltown doctor named Ferrol Sams, who with his wife, Helen, practiced medicine where he had grown up, the farming community of Fayetteville, Georgia. His friends and patients knew Dr. Sams was bright and funny but they didn't dream that he was a novelist. His book, *Run With the Horsemen,* showed them. Mrs. Elliott contracted for it and then became ill, dying of cancer in 1983 shortly after seeing the book through publication. *Run With the Horsemen* justified her faith in it by selling sixty-thousand copies immediately and going into paperback. Dr. Sam's second book, *The Whisper of the River,* was similarly successful, attracting the covetous eyes of New York editors, but love of and loyalty to Peachtree were stronger in Dr. Sams than the enticements of the traditional book publishing business. His third book is to be a Peachtree publication.

Meanwhile, Chuck Perry, who was night managing editor of the *Atlanta Journal* and *Constitution,* was lured away by the Elliott family to take over the post of vice president and executive editor of Peachtree. And the growth has continued.

"When I came Peachtree was publishing seven to nine books a year," Mr. Perry recalled. "In 1986 we'll publish twenty books, and by the end of the year we will have more than a hundred titles in print."

What Helen Elliott may have only intuitively sensed when she began is now obvious to all. As Chuck Perry put it, "The South has always been fertile ground for writers, but the business of publishing was in New York — for no reason except that New York felt it had to be that way. We are evidence contrary to the myth. Southern readers are just like New England readers, if you can get the books to them. When there were fewer urban areas, that wasn't easy. Now the South is a great place to sell books."

Wayne Elliott said there are sixty publishers flourishing in the South now, several in the Atlanta area, in addition to the university presses which have attracted poets and short story writers of notable talent.

Twenty years ago when I undertook to name the published writers in Atlanta, a friend warned me that I could not, without the most grueling census-taking, list them all.

"You can spit in any direction," he said, "and you'll hit a writer."

The task has been compounded out of all reason now. We have book fairs and everybody's engagement calendar includes dropping by a bookstore at least once a week for some dear chum's autographing session. There are clubs and informal groups and classes in writing at the colleges, and many writers are prone to draw nigh to one another for comfort and occasional conviviality. But not all are known to one another because inevitably there are the ones like William Faulkner who are solitary workers.

Alice Walker, who won a Pulitzer prize for her book, *The Color Purple,* was such a one. From rural Eatonton, Georgia, birthplace of Joel Chandler Harris, author of the Uncle Remus stories, she came to Atlanta to teach at Atlanta University, but few members of the writing trade were prepared for the publication of her book and its worldwide acclaim. They rallied to hail her book by giving it Atlanta's Jim Townsend Award for Fiction at a gala party in 1984. (Townsend was the highly popular founding editor of the *Atlanta* magazine, a glossy publication which fostered the talent of many young writers. The award, now sponsored by Georgia State University, honors Townsend's memory and rewards a local author picked out of the year's crop by a New York editor, an agent and an Atlanta critic.) Miss Walker, busy in California, did not attend the awards party in her honor.

The attention given local authors by their peers, by bookstores and reviews and interviews in the newspapers and on radio and television bespeaks the town's friendly attitude toward writers. It was not so many years ago when a Georgia writer named Caroline Miller won the Pulitzer for *Lamb in His Bosom.* Many people loved the book but did not aspire to meet the author or consider feting her with parties. Even Margaret Mitchell, the next Georgia winner of the Pulitzer, had few parties until the movie premiere of "Gone With the Wind." Now the movies are so cognizant of the writing going on in Atlanta that options and contracts from Hollywood come winging in right regularly.

Fortunately, our town is not like New Orleans, of which a bookbuyer once said, a shade ruefully, "People here have better things to do than to read."

Religion, Wild and Juicy

CHAPTER XIII

H.L. Mencken called the South the "Bible belt" and viewed it as a church-going, hymn-shouting and Scripture-thumping region where fundamentalism and blue laws reigned and the pious drank white lightning in the bathroom.

Atlanta, being the capital of the Deep South, would ostensibly be home plate for that kind of religion.

If it is or ever was, it doesn't seem so to the locals now. Atlantans go to church, it's true. Nothing short of a smallpox epidemic would keep the city's more than 1,300 churches from standing-room-only attendance on Sunday, and many of them have double-sessions. (This serves two purposes. It makes room for all comers and it enables churchgoers who want to go to the lake or the golf course to get an early start.)

This came as a surprise to some people who regarded Atlanta as the seat of Southern Methodism and assumed that with so much Methodist activity in the area it had to be the predominant denomination.

In many ways the Methodists have had the public eye — and ear. Emory University is a Methodist college with a finger in many civic pies. Due to the benevolence of the Candler family, ardent

Methodists all, Emory owns a great deal of a real estate. Warren Akin Candler, brother of Asa Griggs Candler, founder of the Coca-Cola Company, was a Methodist bishop and one of the most vocal and most colorful churchmen in the region.

I interviewed Bishop Candler at his home on North Decatur Road on his eighty-fourth birthday, shortly before his death in 1941. He was old and ill, but vestiges of the power and wit which had for more than fifty years dominated the church scene in the South were still present.

Alfred M. Pierce, who wrote the old bishop's biography, *Giant Against the Sky,* called him "master of scorn, ridicule, invective, irony and sarcasm." He set out to be a lawyer, but he also studied theology at Emory College at Oxford, Georgia (the forerunner to the present university and now a junior college). As a result he was licensed to preach, and three months before his eighteenth birthday he was pushed by a classmate into preaching his first sermon.

It must have been a potent experience because, taking the text, "Whatsoever thy hand findeth to do, do it with thy might," young Mr. Candler converted himself. He gave up law forthwith for the ministry. Those who heard him say he was a memorable preacher and a tireless one. Today's fashion for the half-hour sermon would have been abhorrent to him.

"The age of short sermons is the age of shallow piety," he said.

But when he had to sit through a brother preacher's seemingly endless sermon and it came time to announce the closing hymn, Mr. Candler darted a glance full of mischief at the long-winded one and solemnly called for the singing of "Hallelujah, 'Tis Done."

Bishop Candler did not suffer fools gladly, and he was equally merciless with himself. When his members gave him an automobile once and he drove it into the bushes while trying to negotiate his own driveway, a neighbor rushed out and asked him if he was hurt and if she should call the doctor.

"No, call a veterinarian," said the bishop. "If I hadn't been a jackass I wouldn't have been trying to drive that thing."

A short man, five feet, six inches tall, with a massive head and a mighty torso, Bishop Candler was a formidable figure in the pulpit, and the timid tried to avoid provoking his wrath. Once an usher asked a woman to take a crying baby from the sanctuary

while the bishop spoke. The bishop saw her leaving and he interrupted his sermon to call out, "Sit down, my sister! It's a mighty
sorry shepherd that is bothered with the bleating of the lambs!"

The bishop was frequently in conflict with various branches of
the Methodist Church. At the peak of some doctrinal dispute,
according to Pierce, somebody asked Bishop Candler if he didn't
think his opponents were good people.

"Oh, yes," the bishop replied with no great enthusiasm.

The next question was if he didn't think "they will get to
heaven."

"Yes," said Candler, "if they don't run past it."

Bishop Candler served as president of Emory University and as
chancellor. He was named "First Citizen of Atlanta" by the Chamber of Commerce in 1932 and the Emory theology school now
bears his name. He was vigorously opposed to whiskey in any
form, and although he must have been pleased that his brother's
Coca-Cola fortune was poured liberally into Emory, he stoutly
maintained that he owned no stock in the company.

"I never owned any stock except a one-eyed pony and a three-
teat cow," he said.

Understandably partisan about his own denomination, the
bishop had no patience with those who wandered into other folds.
When he learned that one of his students had married and joined the
Episcopal Church with his wife, the bishop said, "I always knew
that if you ever got religion you'd get it in its mildest form."

In common with old-time Methodist evangelists, Bishop Candler believed that a public speech which made no appeal to the
emotions was inherently defective.

The greatest exponent of this brand of emotional oratory to
parallel Bishop Candler's career in the Atlanta area was the sensational Sam Jones, also a Methodist.

Sam Jones, who lived from 1857 to 1906, like Bishop Candler
started out to be a lawyer. He got so far as practicing in the little
town of Cartersville, forty miles north of Atlanta, but as he later
wrote of himself, he was "bad to drink whiskey."

Latter-day chroniclers say the young lawyer's addiction to spirits
wasn't nearly so serious as he pictured it after he quit, but it must
have troubled his family because his father extracted a deathbed

promise from him that he would give it up "and meet me in Heaven."

The young lawyer turned preacher delivered his first sermon at little New Hope church near Cartersville, preaching in the place of the pastor, his grandfather, who came down with a throat malady at the last minute one Sunday. After that he must have sensed his own power, because he was committed to the ministry. He preached all over America, and when he died from a heart attack on a train outside Little Rock, there was national mourning.

His body was brought back to Cartersville for the funeral and then transported to Atlanta by special train, which was draped in black and white with a life-sized picture of him on the front of the engine, to lie in state at the capitol for two days. Thirty thousand people filed past his bier to pay tribute to him.

Walt Holcomb, author of his biography, *Sam Jones: An Ambassador of the Almighty*, traveled and preached with Sam Jones for many years. He wrote of his "merry black eyes," his sense of humor and the "crude, rugged, epigrammatic vigor of what he said."

He quoted Jones himself as saying he never attended a theological "cemetery" and summed up his own brand of preaching by saying, "I always wanted to get the juice out of the text. Others may deal in bones and hoofs and horns and that which is dry and tasteless. I always wanted the juice and always wanted to give the juice to others."

He admitted that he was not "a stickler for creeds, nor an expounder of dogma" but he devoted himself to championing right and denouncing wrong.

One thing he fought hip and thigh (after he himself gave it up) was whiskey.

"Whiskey is a good thing in its place," he said, "but its place is in hell." And another time, "Nobody but a scoundrel will sell whiskey and nobody but a fool will drink it."

The Reverand Mr. Jones was a good administrator and once headed the Methodist Children's Home in Decatur, raising sixty thousand dollars for its support in a brief and eloquent campaign. He was himself a sunny-dispositioned man who liked children. (His son, Paul, was a *Constitution* reporter for many years and two of his grandsons were for many years staff members — Paul, amusements editor, and Howell, telegraph editor. Both are dead now.)

"I have known preachers who looked as sad and solemn as if their father in heaven was dead and hadn't left them a cent," he said.

Once he spoke out against whiskey in a town where liquor interests were powerful and the mayor took his cane to the evangelist. Doffing his clerical dignity, Sam wrested the cane from the man, threw it aside and felled him with his fists.

To the amazed Walt Holcomb he explained, "If I let him whip me, everywhere I went some one-gallused mayor would be jumping on me. I decided to nip that past-time in the bud."

Paul Jones recalled that one of his grandfather's most popular sermons was entitled, "Quit Your Meanness." This was a favorite theme of his. "Most men when they feel mean feel natural," he said. And once in an address to brother preachers he sympathized with them for some of "the animals" in their flock.

"I wonder that some of you preachers do as well as you do," he said, "when I look at the team you have hooked up — a mule, a billygoat, a skunk and a bumblebee . . . the old kicker kicking at everything that comes up, the old butter with his head as hard as a billygoat, the old toper smelling worse than a skunk, and the old long-tongued sister who can sit in the parlor and lick a skillet in the kitchen."

These famous preachers' successors in local pulpits tend to be more sedate and less picturesque. The Presbyterians had for a brief time the famous Peter Marshall at Westminster Presbyterian Church. He met his wife, Catherine, while she was a student at Agnes Scott College, attending his church, and after their marriage they went on to Washington where he gained renown as pastor of the National Presbyterian Church and chaplain of the U.S. Senate. His career has since been delineated in Mrs. Marshall's book *A Man Called Peter* and a movie of the same name, which was filmed largely in Atlanta.

The late Rev. Arthur J. Moore, a bishop emeritus of the Methodist Church, one of the leading churchmen in the country for more than half a century, approached these colorful antecedents in humor and showmanship. Back in the early 1930's, the Methodist Church was "short on bishops," as Bishop Moore used to tell it. They sent him to Asia where he became bishop of three million Methodists. He numbered among his flock Generalissimo Chiang Kai-shek and Madame Chiang, who, as a girl, attended the Methodist Wesleyan College in Macon, Georgia. The Chinese couple remained his friends all their lives and he visited them in 1960, when he retired.

The Methodist Church got its start in Georgia with the arrival of John and Charles Wesley in Savannah from England with General Oglethorpe's founding British colony. Social reform — later formation of labor unions in England — has long been one of its strong points. Bishop Moore was, with Ralph McGill, one of the founders of the Southern Regional Council, an organization established for the improvement of race relations. Although he later withdrew from the council, Bishop Moore said it was not for lack of conviction and considered himself, and the Methodist Church generally, to be liberal on matters of race.

Bishop Moore was a railroad flagman in Waycross, Georgia, when he was converted. With a young man's zeal, he yearned to go immediately to the foreign missionary field. The church board rejected him — twenty years from the time he was to become one of the denomination's really ocean-hopping, globe-circling bishops.

Years later there were many funny stories about the old bishop's worldwide fame. A photographer and I went to meet him when he flew into Atlanta one day after the plane in which he was coming home from China went down in a Kansas wheat field. The pilot asked for a volunteer to go to the nearest farm house and ask for help while he tinkered with the airliner's radio. Bishop Moore, then an old man, hiked sturdily across many acres arriving at the kitchen door of a remote house. The door opened, a shaft of lamp light fell on the stocky, gray-haired man and the housewife cried, "Why, Bishop Moore, come right in."

On the whole, local churchmen are inclined to suspect that religion in Atlanta exists, if not in Bishop Candler's "mildest form," at lease in a milder form than of yore. Sometimes members of the clergy wonder if with age and dignity the churches lose some

Roswell Presbyterian Church, welcoming worshippers since 1840

of the "juice" which was so important to Sam Jones.

This has occurred to the Methodists and Baptists particularly. Traditionally the churches of the working classes, both denominations run heavily these days to solid citizens, big, beautiful, decorator-done church "plants" with general budgets and ministers who, far from being tent hoisters and damnation shouters, belong to the Rotary or Kiwanis Clubs, one or more country clubs, and write books and newspaper columns.

The Atlanta Council of Church sponsors many of the city's good works, including a chaplaincy program at Grady Hospital, where many young ministers intern in the field of medical ministry. There is a Council of Churches social agency in the Community Chest and the Christmas Bureau, operated from Thanksgiving to Christmas as a clearing house for all Yuletide charities. The council also sponsors a refugee resettlement program, a task force on the homeless and maintains emergency help centers which give financial assistance to people who cannot pay their utility bills or buy food and shelter.

The Protestant Radio-Television Center near the Emory campus is an interesting interdenominational project. Here a big staff of professionals works full time producing films and radio tapes for broadcast in all parts of the world. Stars from Hollywood and Broadway frequently come to appear in these productions and recently many of them have been used by the Voice of America.

Of the nineteen million Baptists in America, ten million are Southern Baptists, a group which split with their Yankee brethren at a meeting in Augusta, Georgia, in 1845 over several issues, one being whether slave-owning ministers could be missionaries. Of this ten million, the biggest Protestant denomination in the country, more than 310,731 belong to 422 Greater Atlanta churches.

This doesn't count several-score independent Baptist groups who don't belong to the Southern Baptist Convention. The Baptist, by all accounts, is a ruggedly independent churchman, autonomous in his own congregation, under no compulsion to cotton to or affiliate with any other organization. That's how the term "hardshell" Baptist came about.

The "hardshell" originally was a Baptist who was a unit to himself, holding so firmly to the doctrine of the "priest-hood of the believer" that he permitted no minister in his church and eschewed all missionary work. There are several "hardshell" or Primitive Baptist churches in Atlanta, some new ones with beautiful modern churches, and although they vary in their operations, some still observe the old foot-washing rites and some cling to the custom of having no minister and no instrumental music in the church.

Contrast this kind of Baptist with the Southern Baptist's impressive Second Ponce de Leon Church. (It started out on Ponce de Leon but has been next door to the Roman Catholic Cathedral of Christ the King on Peachtree for many years.) Second Ponce de Leon has a rich and stylish congregation numbering four thousand members and regularly contributes a quarter of a million dollars to missions.

Baptists as a denomination have been criticized for failure to take a positive liberal stand on racial matters in Atlanta. Some of this criticism, says Jack Hardwell of the denomination's paper, *The Christian Index,* is justified but understandable.

"No one person or organization speaks for a Baptist," he explained. "The convention merely suggests or recommends and individual churches and members are by no means bound by its action. That's why we call our representatives in the convention 'messengers' instead of delegates. They can vote without binding the people back home."

The Christian Index itself has been more outspoken. In times of racial dispute, it has repeatedly reminded Baptists that the Christian approach is one of law and order and "respect for the rights and humanity of all races." It fights gambling and illicit liquor traffic tooth and nail. It also campaigned to have a Negro student from Ghana admitted to the Baptist Mercer University in Macon.

The paper is now edited by Mr. Hardwell and is one of the oldest (founded in 1822) in America. The late Dr. Louie D. Newton, long-time pastor of the Druid Hills Baptist Church, edited the *Index* for ten years.

Dr. Newton, sometimes a controversial figure in Atlanta and a particularly strident voice where alcoholic beverages are concerned, was the dean of Baptist preachers in the area and sometimes called "Mister Baptist" by his colleagues. He was a former president of the Southern Baptist Convention and former vice-president of the Baptist World Alliance and in 1953 was named America's "Clergyman of the Year."

When he died in June 1986, a week before his beloved Southern Baptist Convention was to convene in Atlanta, friends and fellow pastors kept vigil around his hospital bed.

The Rev. Paul Mims, who succeeded Dr. Newton as pastor of the three-thousand member Druid Hills Baptist church, said, "We were just standing around his bed and we had just sung 'Amazing Grace,' which was one of his favorite hymns, and he just kind of smiled and closed his eyes."

When Company Comes

Although it loves visitors and frequently gets exercised over what has come to be referred to as "tourism," a well-paying industry which has replaced cotton and corn as a money crop, Atlanta is not really a tourist town. Its resemblance to a bonafide tourist place like New Orleans, for instance, is about as close as that of a man who built a better mousetrap to Disney World.

People beat a pathway to our door, all right, but their mission is usually business and not to see the sights. While they are here Atlantans want them to have a good time and diligently stir around, pointing out the resident's routine delights, hoping to more than compensate for the shortage of sight-seeing buses and guides giving step-this-way-folks spiels.

It must work out so the visitor doesn't feel unduly deprived, because I know a long-time resident of Atlanta whose advice to all brides is, "If you're going to live here, my dear, don't have a guest room unless you want it eternally filled. No matter where your relatives and friends are going, Atlanta is on the way."

To some visitors, usually wives accompanying their husbands on a business trip or to a convention, the department stores downtown and at half a dozen malls, where almost every store you ever heard of from the locals to such name establishments as Nieman-Marcus, Saks Fifth Avenue and Lord and Taylor have shops, are tourist attraction enough. A visiting executive recently reported to his brethren at a convention that his wife had been "lost in Rich's for three days."

"I wonder," he mused aloud, "if anybody has ever sued a department store for alienation of affections."

Groups with special interests are the easiest to entertain. Garden clubbers hit the flower shows and garden tours, of which there are many in the spring and fall. Music lovers, if they are lucky enough to get tickets, aim for one of the concerts which abound in season, the Symphony or Music Club series. Antiquers will case the local shops and galleries, and make one of the auctions, which are held almost nightly. If their timing is right, they'll also get to one of the quarterly Southeastern Antiques Shows at the Civic Center. There are boating shows at the Merchandise Mart, and Civil War buffs come primed for centennial fetes and celebrations. Gospel singers have all-night sing fests, and once I lucked into a chance interview with a group of wide-eyed young people, students of a northern morticians' college, who were making their senior class trip to the Atlanta Casket Company and H. M. Patterson's famous undertaking emporium, Spring Hill.

What Atlanta has to offer the visitor obviously depends upon what the visitor is interested in.

The first thing nearly everybody does with a guest is to drive through the northside sections where the more splendid homes are situated. This is gratifying to us hosts, who never tire of seeing how the other, well-heeled half lives. And I think guests find it interesting because not all cities house their rich people in palaces set in parks.

In the 1920's and 1930's, Atlanta money literally went to the woods. Out on West Paces Ferry Road and half a dozen others, Norman castles and Italian villas and English manor houses came to what had previously been sourwood thickets, broom-sedge fields and forests of oak, maple and pine. Everybody who built a big house in those days had acreage to show it off and they used it profligately. Landscape design supplemented freehanded nature with fountains and terraces, arbors and rose gardens and statuary.

The magnificent Swan House, home of the Atlanta Historical Society

Some of these old estates are already doomed. One of the great ones, built by Robert F. Maddox, the former banker and one-time mayor, was sold to the state as a site for a new and totally different governor's mansion. The Andrew Calhoun home, an Italian villa called "The Pink Palace" by generations of Atlantans, was set roughly a morning's hike from the road, and Sunday drivers used to park their cars at the big double gates and gaze upon it with awe and admiration. Now, alas, its grounds have been cut up into subdivision lots and the winding roadway to the palace is lined with ranch houses.

There are still many palaces and near-palaces on West Paces Ferry, Habersham, Wesley, Andrews and neighboring roads — and for as long as they last they are among our town's most reliable attention-getters.

The second thing I try to show every visitor is the Cyclorama in Grant Park.

This curious old painting, housed in its own circular building in the city park, not too far from the elephant house and the rest of the zoo, is an unbeatable combination of art show, sideshow and

A scene from the Battle of Atlanta as depicted in the Cyclorama

history lesson. I had lived in Atlanta many years before I got around to seeing it, and then I went in line of duty. Olivia de Havilland, the screen Melanie of *Gone With the Wind*, considered it so memorable she brought her first husband, author Marcus Goodrich, by Atlanta on their wedding trip just to see it. A photographer and I went to the park to cover their visit, and I have been going back with visitors on an average of once a year since.

The picture, fifty feet high and four hundred feet in circumference, depicts the Battle of Atlanta. It was painted about twenty years after the battle by a group of German artists and taken on a tour of the United States in the 1880's. It dropped from sight for a couple of years and then showed up in Atlanta in 1892, where it was eventually sold at auction to George U. Gress, a citizen who presented it to the city. I don't know what they did with this eighteen-thousand-pound behemoth until it got its own building in Grant Park in 1921, but in 1936 the WPA took a hand and, lo and behold, the old picture went three-dimensional and was wired for sound.

The foreground was filled in with blasted tree trunks, broken rails and crossties and plaster figures of soldiers, all so cunningly constructed and lighted that the visitor seated in the auditorium which revolves slowly and imperceptibly, has a sensation of being in the midst of battle.

The ladies of the Cyclorama staff used to give little speeches explaining the battle action, but now the narrative is taped and as the story unfolds, the point of the battle being described is subtly lighted on the canvas. All this with musical accompaniment and the sound of musket and cannot fire. Then the lights go up and they play "Dixie" and you come blinking out into the sunshine feeling like Scarlett O'Hara the morning after the battle.

On the ground floor there is a newly refurbished museum with a computer which puts the history buff in touch with what was happening on any date during the war. You punch in the day, month and year in which you are interested and there is unfolded for you the details of the battle. The locomotive engine, the Texas, star of the Disney movie, "The Great Locomotive Chase," is the premier exhibit here, richly supplemented by thousands of photographs, old letters, swords and shells and uniforms. Here also is a model of the cruiser "Atlanta," rebuilt by public subscription after it was torpedoed in the Pacific in World War II.

Akin to the cyclorama as a sight and wonder spectacularly and peculiarly Atlanta — that is, not to be seen anywhere else in the world — is Stone Mountain.

Although it is in another county (DeKalb) with another municipality at its base (Stone Mountain, Georgia, once called New Gibraltar), Atlantans have for more than a century had a funny, compulsive attachment to this monstrous old chunk of granite. When nothing much is happening — and sometimes when there's plenty happening — Atlantans do battle over Stone Mountain.

It has been the center of outrageous civic argument, the victim of one national money-grabbing scandal, the object of fervent patriotic hopes and aspirations and, betimes, chipped at, dynamited, carved, hauled off by the trainload, surveyed, landscaped and, above all, climbed.

On any sunny weekend you can find hundreds of families trudging up Stone Mountain. For years teen-agers ended their high school dances by racing out to the mountain, taking off their shoes and clambering up its worn gray granite flank. Elias Nour, a refrigerator repairman, lived his life in the shadow of the mountain and explored it so thoroughly that he was always being called upon to rescue some foolhardy or unwary climber from a cliff or crevice. This started when he was thirteen years old, and the score totaled thirty-six rescues before he retired and moved to Florida. People have been killed in falls from the mountain. Suicides have leaped from it. It was once the favorite rallying ground of the Ku Klux Klan. (Where could you find a better vantage point for burning a cross than a big bare stone pinnacle rising 1,586 feet above sea level?) The Venable family, then owners of the mountain, finally stopped these gatherings after one of the KKK's noisier "Konvokations."

Old Stone Mountain has been a variety of things to a variety of people. The Indians who used to hold their council meetings there are said to have looked on the mountain with superstitious awe. General George Washington's aides found it a likely spot for military conference. Quarrymen who shipped out millions of tons of it to build such Atlanta institutions as the Federal Penitentiary, Courthouse, Library and churches, as well as hundreds of post offices all over the United States and in Cuba, have called it "the largest deposit of merchantable granite in the world."

The United Daughters of the Confederacy, who started trying to make it a Confederate memorial back in 1915, called it a "custodian of imperishable glory." Geologists have said it was "born in the nether fires of the earth" and older than the Pyrenees, the Rockies or the Himalayas. Frank Daniel, a *Journal* writer who had observed its misadventures for nearly half a century, once called it "a memorial to Georgia chicanery." And Atlanta's Mayor Ivan Allen, officiating at the launching of a cable car to the summit, called the mountain the only thing about Atlanta "Sherman didn't burn or the Yankee carpetbaggers cart away."

Periodically, Atlantans retell the history of old Stone Mountain, relating with relish the apocryphal tale of how it was sold sight unseen to an Athens, Georgia, man years ago. When he arrived to claim it he was so shaken by what he had acquired he quickly swapped it for a mule and a pair of shoes and went home. An Augusta woman tells how her ancestors bought it for forty dollars and a pony, and there's also the story of an early owner who offered to trade the mountain for a long-barreled shotgun and a silk handkerchief but could find no takers.

In any case, records show that Sam and William Venable bought it for forty-eight thousand dollars in 1887 and it cost the State of Georgia a cool million dollars "and other valuable considerations" when it was acquired for a state park in 1959. For years Scotch and Welsh quarrymen offered the principal activity on the mountain, but in 1916 the United Daughters of the Confederacy acquired the steep side for a Confederate memorial. The Venable family deeded this chunk of the mountain and some level land in front of it to the UDC with the stipulation that if a memorial was not completed in twelve years it would revert to the family.

The memorial, needless to say, was not completed. The sculptor Gutzon Borglum started the first carving on the mountain, a mammoth, two-hundred-foot-high procession of men, guns and horses with Robert E. Lee, Stonewall Jackson and Jefferson Davis riding in the foreground and columns of Confederate infantry swinging off in the distance.

World War I interrupted the work, but it was resumed in 1922 with funds raised by an especially minted U.S. half dollar which the UDC sold for one dollar. In 1924 the head of General Lee was unveiled with some ceremony — and then the memorial hit the skids.

Money was going fast, the carving was going slow. Mr. Borglum was dismissed, and in a rage of righteous indignation he destroyed his model and fled the city before an injunction. Subsequent investigation vindicated the sculptor and involved the president of the Stone Mountain Association in misuse of funds. Clark Howell, editor of the Atlanta *Constitution,* later pointed out that as long as "the Daughters" were running the thing themselves it went fine, but when a board of Atlanta businessmen took over to help them the project broke down.

Augustus Lukeman was the second sculptor hired, and he began by blasting the heads off Lee and Jackson and starting over. On April 9, 1928, the memorial association issued engraved invitations to an unveiling of "General Robert E. Lee and Traveler" on the sixty-third anniversary of Appomattox. Two years later

Lukeman discontinued work because of lack of funds, and in 1932 he died.

Time and the weather eroded the unfinished figures. Weeds grew up at the base of the mountain where a landscaped plaza with a reflecting pool had been planned. People spoke sadly of "the unfinished memorial" but continued to climb the mountain, picnic in its shadow and take visitors to view the carving through a telescope at the dilapidated little concession stand at the base of the mountain, where you could buy Cokes and postcards.

Some citizens, however, never relinquished the dream of having Stone Mountain recognized by the whole world as "the Eighth Wonder," which Georgians have always called it. Scott Candler, for many years the DeKalb County commissioner, secured an option on two thousand acres of the mountain from the Venable heirs and later, as director of the State Department of Commerce, he was able to give impetus to the park plan.

Things have been moving fast since then. The Stone Mountain Park Authority was formed and empowered to issue five million dollars' worth of bonds to make the old mountain "the scenic showplace of the South." A ten-thousand-dollar competition was launched to find an artist to finish the memorial, and a sculptor named Walter Hancock was chosen from a field of nine. Crews moved in to build highways around the mountain, a five-mile scenic railroad, dams and a five-hundred-acre lake.

Members of the authority scouted the state with the idea of assembling in the three-thousand-acre park area everything, both old and new, primitive and civilized, which might interest visitors to the South. By the spring of 1963 they were well along in accomplishing this goal. Home folks trooped out to the mountain by the thousand every fair Sunday to cheer the project on. And as one visitor happily noted, "It's going to be glorious — a sort of cross between Williamsburg, Disneyland and the Grand Canyon."

There's a mountaintop observatory with restaurant, a cable car (Swiss-built and appropriately dedicated by cracking both a bottle of Swiss wine and a bottle of Coca-Cola on its prow), a whole antebellum plantation layout, complete with white-columned "great house," overseer's cottage, slave cabins, outbuildings, country store and gardens. These buildings were moved bodily from older sections of Georgia and lovingly rebuilt and furnished with antiques of the period.

There's a side-wheel showboat on the lake, a railroad museum, a game ranch, where you can get a close-up of buffalo and the deer come and eat out of your hand. There's an old car museum, a grist mill where you can buy water-ground meal, picnic areas and campsites.

The aim of the authority is to give the visitor something for his money — if he has money to spend — but to give him something anyhow. Many of the attractions are free, including a battle museum where Sherman's march to the sea is refought with lights on a vast relief map. Picnicking and camping and fishing from the bank are all free. And so, of course, is climbing.

The railroad trip is perhaps the most Disneylandish touch of all. The little train, called General II, after that one in "The Great Locomotive Chase," chugs around the mountain with bell ringing and whistle blowing. Two villages, one patterned with a pioneer North Georgia settlement and the other a make-believe Indian village, have been built on the route, and when the train passes, raids and massacres break out with musketry cracking and arrows flying. Delighted young passengers are invited to bring their own six-shooters from home to "help fight off the attackers." These attackers are, of course, war-painted locals, but they fling themselves into the fray with satisfying realism.

Stone Mountain is fifteen miles from downtown Atlanta, and the old streetcar which used to careen wildly and inexpensively out from town has long since vanished.

In recent years Atlanta has become very nearly a town for walking tours and, of course, there are bus tours of the kind you find in New York, San Francisco, New Orleans and Charleston. Local citizens walk with pleasure, considering it enough to be abroad in the city, savoring its routine sight and smells. But unless the downtown restaurants and stores and theaters are your destination, you can count on covering distances, sometimes great distances, to see the homes and historic shrines and recreation spots which are beloved by the home folks.

If you don't have a car and don't want to bestir yourself to get out of the downtown area, you can still have a pleasant enough time.

On weekdays the state capitol is open and there's no better place to get a quick briefing on state history than from monument-reading on the lawn, which, incidentally, happens to be one of the prettiest and best tended yards in town. (The late Secretary of State Ben Fortson was so zealous about velvety lawn and year-round blooming borders that during the bitter winter of 1962-63 when everything froze, he invested in six hundred dollars' worth of green dye to restore color to the brown grass.) The second floor of the capitol houses the state's Hall of Fame, and although marble busts and dark portraits of dead heroes are not everybody's dish, some of us feel one way to appraise a community is to take a look at the men it has most admired.

The third floor of the capitol is given over mostly to its legislative halls — a great show, in season, and free, unless you count the cost to the taxpayer. And the fourth floor has a small museum which never fails to waylay me when I pass. It depicts the state's natural and economic assets with glass cases full of agricultural and geological exhibits, Indian relics and jewel stones, mammoth cotton plants and birds and insects, stuffed animals and snakes.

If you are not a glass-case tourist, a plaque and monument reader, or a peerer at portraits, you will know it and skip this. But if you've never been able to tell a mockingbird from a field lark or a rattlesnake from a copperhead, if you're curious about kaolin mines, shrimp boats, pulpwood or Indian pottery, you can spend happy and profitable hours here without cost.

The capitol is within walking distance of most downtown hotels or you can step on a MARTA train and get off on the ground floor of a state office building across the street from it. If you are planning a trip to Atlanta, you can write ahead for information about sights and wonders within a day's drive of Atlanta — or beyond, if you have time — from the Tourist Division of the Department of Industry and Trade, P.O. Box 1776, Atlanta 30301. Or if you want to drop in when you arrive in town, their office is not in the capitol but in Suite 605 at 230 Peachtree Street, NW.

For a start there's the 159-mile round trip which will take you to the Warm Springs Foundation of polio fame and, of course, the charmingly simple cottage which was President Roosevelt's "Little White House." This is now a state park and has been preserved substantially as it was the day he died there, April 12, 1945. There's a museum on the grounds with many mementos of his days as president and part-time Georgian. The Warm Springs tour also includes a trip to President Roosevelt's favorite lookout on Pine Mountain, where he grilled steaks for guests and neighbors; visits to a trio of pretty little towns and two gardens — Callaway Gardens, built as a vacation spot with food and lodging and activities, and Dunaway Gardens, twenty acres of flowers and trees.

Another tour is north through Civil War battlefield country and some remarkable sites of Indian restoration, including New Echota, the capital of the Cherokee Nation and the Etowah Indian Mounds in the mineral belt section near Cartersville (round trip 248 miles).

A third tour swings by Stone Mountain to take in Athens, the site of the University of Georgia and several other beautiful little towns which are, like Athens, notable for the high incidence of their Greek Revival architecture. This one brings you back by Conyers, which is about twenty-four miles southeast of Atlanta and is distinguished in this predominantly Protestant countryside for its exotic neighbors, the Trappist monks. These solemn fellows in their brown cowls came to Georgia from Gethsemane, Kentucky, in 1944 to build a monastery on some cottoned-out land, part of which once belonged to the silent-era screen star, Colleen Moore. Although quiet and unsmiling and foreign to this part of the world, the monks became cherished citizens in this little suburban community. They vote and contribute to charities and run such a model farm that it has been an inspiration to their neighbors. Their dairy and bread trucks cover the countryside, distributing rich milk and the fragrant dark brown loaves for which they are famous. They have designed and built a beautiful church where numbers of Atlantans go on Easter and Christmas to sit in the balcony and listen to the ancient Gregorian chants. Visitors are welcome to parts of the monastery, and next to their bread, which I always buy, I like to visit the greenhouse and come away with a few pots of the heart-leafed and silver-edged monastery ivy.

A fourth one-day tour covers 218 miles, round trip, and takes you into the mountains, the gold-mining country around

Dahlonega, where the first major gold rush began in 1828 and where tourists are still invited to pan for gold. It also covers more battlefields and antebellum homes. In the same journey you may visit Helen, a simple Georgia mountain town which was transformed into an alpine village a decade or so ago and now draws roughly three million visitors a year to its souvenir shops and restaurants and motels. Cleveland, through which you will pass, is also the home of the wildly popular Cabbage Patch doll hospital, a favorite stop for little girls especially.

If you have more time to spend and would like to travel farther, the state Chamber of Commerce can fix you up with plans for seven tours which come close to covering the whole varied big state — from the mountains to the sea, from the peach orchards to the vast brooding Okefenokee Swamp on the Florida border.

I think it is typical of Atlanta, but perhaps not exclusive in these days of fast freeways and winged traffic, that its all-embracing civic pride reaches so far out into the state. The lakes, Allatoona and Lanier, are by no means Atlanta lakes. The closest their shores come to Atlanta is about thirty miles, but every weekend of the summer thousands of Atlantans are at one or the other of them water-skiing, swimming, sailing, houseboating, fishing.

The mountains seem closer because on certain afternoons when the atmosphere is right if you look from a viaduct or any other open space in downtown Atlanta, you can see where they begin with the blue shape of Kennesaw against the sky. And when you head north from the city limits, before you are even out of the county, there are whole ranges of mountains stretched out against the horizon in indigo humps and peaks. I am enchanted with the mountains, a section of the state which, until the roads opened up and the power lines came in the 1930's, was virtually untouched by the twentieth century.

Today many Atlantans have weekend or summer places in the hill country and are within reach of the still-secluded hollows and cover where old ways of life and old skills still prevail. Change has come, of course, and the little mountain towns have as many Rexall drugstores and as much neon and pink asbestos siding as little towns anywhere.

But if you wander from the main thoroughfares, you can find

cabin-made, handloomed pretties to admire and sometimes buy. There are still old-time artisans making "settin' chairs" and bottoming them with split white oak, still potters who will "throw" you a churn or a fat cream pitcher on their own wheel and fire them in a kiln which turns Georgia clay from plum red to muted brown or blue.

All across the top of the state there are roads leading through unbelievably beautiful valleys and over swift-running streams lined in springtime with banks of rosy mountain laurel and rhododendron. There are lookouts and picnic spots and a few old-time country inns where the food is still served family style and platters of fried chicken, ham and red-eye gravy and country steak circulate up and down the table with platoons of homegrown vegetables, hot biscuits, cornbread, homemade butter and buttermilk and a minimum of three kinds of honey and six kinds of preserves.

Because the Indians so recently inhabited this country — they were driven west in the infamous "Trail of Tears" in 1834 — Atlanta children are perhaps the premier Indian artifact collectors in the eastern half of the nation. If you don't find Indian arrowheads and shards of Indian pottery in your own backyard, you don't have to travel far to find them. In the last few decades there has been a big effort to restore the remnants of Indian civilization. The Ocmulgee National Monument with mounds and a strange council house in Macon (one hundred miles to the south) are famous. The Etowah Mounds near Cartersville (forty miles to the north) are part of a state park.

New Echota, capital of the peace-loving, highly intelligent and agrarian Cherokee Nation, has been undergoing research and restoration by a team of archeologists for several years. (This is near Calhoun, seventy miles north.) And the home of the Scotch-Cherokee chieftains, James and Joseph Vann, is an unfailing marvel to visitors who thought all Indian chiefs lived in wigwams. This is an elegant brick house, modified Georgian in design, planned for the Vanns by a European architect and handsomely furnished with European imports about 1804. The Georgia Historical Society saved the old house from destruction by time and vandals a few years ago and restored it to its former glory with its elaborate carvings, cantilevered stairway and wainscoting painted

The Jimmy Carter Presidential Library opened in 1986

in the colors of the North Georgia landscape — blue sky, red clay, green trees and yellow ripened grain.

The Vann House, about ninety miles north of Atlanta, is open daily to tourists for a small fee.

There are numbers of Atlantans, of course, who never think of wandering so far afield. They are content to live in city apartments, perhaps one of the new ones which are rearing up among downtown office buildings these days. They can pass up the daisy-starred meadows of the hill country for flowers blooming on traffic islands or in the Citizens and Southern Bank's window boxes. They might drive occasionally to Smyrna, just over the line in Cobb County, to eat country victuals at Aunt Fanny's Cabin, a real old slave shack which has been meticulously kept slanty-shanty primitive, with hot hoecake type cuisine and pickaninnies singing and the whole place knee-deep in visiting movie stars and other celebrities.

This type Atlantan doesn't like to buck traffic, and he doesn't figure he has to, to see some pretty satisfactory sights. After all, the city where once the only truly inspired cooks were in somebody's kitchen has become a city of restaurants. You can eat a Barker's hotdog in Robert Woodruff's pretty little park at Five Points, take a sandwich there from Carlyle's half a block away or catch the turnip pot likker at Mary Mac's tearoom out on Ponce de Leon, if plain inexpensive fare is your choice. If you are feeling like something more elegant, there are three highly regarded restaurants at Buckhead, specializing in continental cuisine. Their names: 103 West (its West Paces Ferry address, of course), Ma Maison and Pano's and Paul's. Our Saturday paper has a supplement which is a gold mine of information on the city's restaurants, as well as other attractions. Beginning with Acadian-Creole, it covers the range of ethnic and American eating places for six or eight pages, ending with Thai food. You can have catfish and barbecue, curry from an Indian chef or get Russian cuisine from four-star Nickolai's Roof atop the Atlanta Hilton.

Either way, I say, you can't lose.

"Singing Hymns and Balling the Jack"

CHAPTER XIV

It was a moment surprising and touching to newcomers to Atlanta, that moment in a little space of quiet when they would suddenly realize they were hearing the town's heartbeat. That moment is no more.

It might have happened in the daytime but it was likely to have happened in the middle of the night when the surf-like pounding of traffic on Peachtree Street had slowed to a meek, ebb-tide whisper. Then you would be aware of a deep low beat, rhythmic as breathing, repetitious as a Bach fugue.

This was the sound of Atlanta's trains.

Now one of the biggest and busiest airports in the world has all but silenced the trains, but many Atlantans remember.

The city was bound around and crisscrossed with railroad tracks, and no matter what else was happening there were always trains moving, cars coupling, switch engines bustling about the yards like suburban housewives too intent on the duties of home to chafe at the clothesline tether of domesticity. Over and above these steady workaday noises there was a recurring theme, the sweet lifted halloo of an arriving freight, coming in from Chicago with snow on its top, the barnyard-fragrant "Pork Chop Special" pulling a load of pigs to the packinghouse siding, the deep-throated peal of a fast passenger heading north with time to make up.

Atlanta was the largest railroad center in the South, with seven systems operating thirteen main lines through the city. More than two hundred and fifty merchandise and package cars originated in and moved out of Atlanta daily, and the Railway Express Agency transported in and out of Atlanta more express shipments per capita than any other city in the United States — an average of five thousand cars per month.

Now one passenger train comes to Atlanta, the Amtrak out of New York and Washington. Only two railroad systems remain and there are no colorful crowded downtown railroad depots any more. They were demolished despite public protest several years ago, leaving only the elegant little Brookwood Station out Peachtree Road as the arrival and departure point for Atlanta passengers. The closest thing to railroad travel for most Atlantans, however, is almost a plaything — which travels around the city on a eighteen-mile belt line several days a week, for the benefit of visitors and poor benighted Atlanta children who were born too late to know about railroads.

This came about because Steve Polk, director of the Georgia Building Authority, could not bear to see the ancient Georgia Railroad depot, not used for passenger service for nearly a century, torn down. State-owned, it is the oldest building in downtown Atlanta and the home base of what they named the New Georgia railroad line, which began its runs behind a seventy-six-year-old coal-fire steam engine in 1985. During the first year and a half, more than thirty-thousand people boarded the New Georgia to see and hear about historic sites from a taped spiel by historian Franklin Garrett. On occasion it runs to Stone Mountain and little Georgia towns with craft fairs and leaf-looking celebrations in the fall.

As Sherman wrote after the war: "Atlanta was like my hand. The palm was the city or hub. The fingers were its spokes — in this case the railroads. I knew that if I could destroy those railroads, the last link of the Confederacy would be broken."

The railroads which brought down fire and destruction on its head also helped in its rebuilding. And although recent years have taken a toll in passenger trains, causing old Atlantans to mourn, the old affection for railroads and railroading is still with us. Old-timers are not reconciled, of course, to the passage of the steam engine — no more than the old-timers before them were reconciled to the loss of the famous old woodburners who employed firemen, engineer and wood passer in the cab and are said to have screamed like souls in torment when they were converted to coal. (This screaming, very real and traceable to mechanical causes, is said to have terrified people as far as forty-miles from the railroad tracks in the late 1870's. The converted engines were called "the screaming girls.")

The loss of the steam whistle is both deeply personal and civic, for most Atlantans grew up on stories of the virtuosity of engines and engineers the way lovers of the Met know the special nuances of a Caruso or a Galli-Curci. And to have Atlanta's steam whistles replaced by the mechanical whistles of the diesel engine was a municipal calamity on a par with having every mocking bird in Piedmont Park struck dumb in his prime.

Still Atlantans love the railroads and the trains and band themselves into what amounts to fan clubs dedicated to the adulation of the Iron Horse. The success of old 290 is an example.

A few years ago E.M. Ivie, a retired Southern engineer and dean of a little group of railroad fans who gathered daily at Union Station to bask in the sweet familiarity of railroad sights and sounds, became alarmed that coming generations might never see or hear a steam engine. Mr. Ivie's alarm spread to the late Leo Aikman, columnist for the Atlanta *Constitution,* and from Leo it fanned out into the state, reaching epidemic proportions. Poor, ignorant children, mourned the railroad devotees, to be reared in deprivation and silence unbroken save by the crude sounds of the jet and diesel age.

They immediately launched a movement to get a proper engine. Not a "cute" historic relic like the famed "Texas," which is in the Civil War museum at the Cyclorama in Grant Park, but a sleek and powerful modern engine. J. Clyde Mixon, president of the Atlanta and West Point Railroad, came forward. His line would contribute an engine they had planned to scrap — the noble 290, which was in main-line passenger service between Atlanta and Montgomery from 1926 to 1954.

The city accepted the train and immediately made plans for placing it on display at Lakewood Park. But the problem of getting the engine from the nearest railroad to the park, a distance of several miles, temporarily baffled Messrs. Ivie and Aikman and others who led the movement. After all, the railroad was sacrificing the scrap value of the engine, a staggering sum of seventy thousand dollars. It could hardly be expected to lay a track to move it. The City Parks Department knew nothing about moving trains.

Leo Aikman cast about for somebody who did know the subject. A luncheon companion suggested the Army, and a few weeks later, with the flags flying and bands playing and hundreds of excited citizens there to cheer them on, the boys of the 836th Engineers Battalion (heavy construction) of the U.S. Army Reserves moved old 290, a few rails at a time, out Pryor Road to Lakewood Park. When the Southeastern Fair opened some weeks later, she had been wired for sound and was the hit of the exposition.

Since the closing of Lakewood Park, 290 has been sent to Duluth to be rejuvenated and put back in service on the New Georgia system.

Visitors are sometimes puzzled to hear Atlantans speaking of "catching the Nancy to Savannah" or "riding the Man to Columbus." Far from being a brand of civic jive talk, these references have their roots in the town's history.

The "Nancy to Savannah" simply refers to the Central of Georgia's streamliner, Nancy Hanks II, and the "Man to Columbus" is another Central shoppers and commuters special, the Man o' War. Both were named for racehorses.

When the Nancy Hanks service to Savannah was reinstated in the late 1940's after an intermission of fifty-odd years, the Central of Georgia found it expedient to take an ad to remind customers that the new streamliner had been named for one of America's most glamorous trains, Nancy Hanks I. And *that* Nancy had been named for one of the swiftest trotting horses in the world.

"Then you *didn't* name the train for Abraham Lincoln's mother?" I said to a railroad man, disappointed that a little story I'd had in mind had blown up.

"Oh, was that *her* name?" asked the railroad executive mildly. "How fast could she run?"

My information on the track performance of Mrs. Lincoln (neé Hanks) was sadly lacking, but the railroad official more than made up for it with figures on the other Nancy Hanks. The racehorse, for instance, a six-year-old bay mare, broke the world's trotting record in 1892 with 2:04 a mile, holding it until 1894 when a horse named Alix dethroned her by a quarter of a second. But in the meantime the Central had named a magnificent train in honor of the dazzling trotter, Nancy Hanks — the first complete train in America to be given a name, although engines had been christened before.

The Nancy was placed in service between Atlanta and Savannah on January 22, 1893, and all of Georgia swelled with pride. Deducting time for stops, she made the 294-mile run to the coast in six hours!

She was royal blue trimmed in gold leaf from her cow catcher to her tail light with likenesses of the horse blown into the frosted-glass panels of the coaches. Even the engine and tender were blue and gold and the crew, although wearing the railroad man's traditional blue denim, had specially cut jackets instead of overalls and blue and gold colored leather caps with the name "Nancy Hanks" emblazoned on the bills.

According to historian Garrett, who is also a railroad fan, the conductor, B.J. (Handsome Barney) Cubbedge was a fitting equerry for this elegant equipage. He wore a white vest with pearl buttons, and when he took up a ticket he lifted his hat with a sweeping bow and made a pretty speech of thanks.

All along the line the country people went out of their way to "see the Nancy go by" and even in the more blasé circles in Atlanta a favorite Sunday afternoon entertainment called for driving out to Fort McPherson for the same — "to see the Nancy go by."

They even made up a song which Mr. Garrett quotes:

> *Some Folks say the Nancy can't run*
> *But stop! Let me tell you what the Nancy done:*
> *She left Atlanta at half past one*
> *And got to Savannah at the setting of the sun.*
> *The Nancy she run so fast*
> *She burnt the wind and scorched the grass!*

Unhappily, the Nancy ran so fast she also "scorched" vast numbers of cattle and hogs and was so glamorous nobody wanted to ride any other train. So after fighting this double handicap for seven months, the Central regretfully retired the first railroad Nancy. At the close of World War II another Nancy, a modest streamliner built to accommodate shoppers and commuters at budget fares, was placed in service but later retired.

As railroads gave Atlanta birth and have shaped her history, so have they contributed to her social life. Mrs. Mulligan, wife of a railroad laborer, gave the town's first party, you recall, and in 1842 the citizens of Terminus laid aside their duties and took off to cheer the departure of the first Western and Atlantic train for Marietta. After that, such ceremonies occurred with a fair amount of regularity, but Atlantans never became jaded by the sight of arriving or departing trains.

On a summer day the old Bankhead Avenue bridge overlooking Inman Yards drew family cars packed with children, come to wave at the trains.

Wherever old-timers gather, the talk is well seasoned with references to such trains as "The Goober," the Georgia Railroad's Atlanta-to-Social Circle special, which was taken off in 1930. It got its name because, according to local raconteurs, tons of goober peanuts were consumed between Social Circle and Atlanta and the aisles were knee-deep in shells. The Air Line Belle, which ran between Atlanta and Toccoa from 1879 to 1931, was famous because it made thirty-nine stops in its ninety-three minute run.

The men who drove the trains were colorful, and some of them met daily with Mr. Ivie and other retired railroaders in the Union Station waiting room for years.

Those who remember and long to preserve some part of railroad history are now members of the Atlanta chapter of the National Railway Historical Society, an active group who run regular steam engine tours to the mountains in the fall and sponsor a railroad museum at Duluth.

Among the most colorful in the gallery of railroad men was the late David J. Fant, who lived to be ninety-odd and was in demand as a speaker at church meetings.

He began preaching while he was an engineer, taking as his

credo the Biblical admonition, "Trust in the Lord." Uncle Dave, or Daddy Fant, as he was sometimes called, drove a beautifully groomed mountain-type locomotive on the Southern. Its front was ornamented with a picture of an open Bible, across which were emblazoned the words: "Holy Bible. Thy Word is Truth. John 17:17."

Mr. Fant was careful to kneel in prayer before every run, and chroniclers of the day called his 153-mile run a "153-mile prayer and sermon." He even prayed for the notorious Bill Miner gang when four of its members flagged him down at White Sulphur Springs, Georgia, and robbed his train of $127,000 in cash, which was being transported between New Orleans and New York. The robbers were caught and jailed within a week and Daddy Fant called on them in their cells and knelt and prayed with them.

All along the line between Greenville, South Carolina, and Atlanta his fans marked his passage and marveled at his speed. In the fashion of the day they committed his feat to rhyme:

We can tell by the way she'll roar and rant
If the man at the throttle is Daddy Fant!

One night the engineer was making up time and, as Charles H. Dickey wrote in the Atlanta *Journal* magazine in 1935: "He turned the steam onto the pistons until the white drive wheels revolved so rapidly they all but seemed to be standing still. The fireman, yelling across the end of the boiler, said, 'Daddy, ain't we batting 'em up too fast tonight?' From the other side of the reeling cab the engineer intoned sonorously: 'Trust in the Lord!' "

It was the era of the railroad evangelist, who sang hymns as he broke new speed records. Freight engines were called "jacks" and many an engineer was famed for "singing hymns and balling the jack."

An older and ill-fated contemporary of Daddy Fant's was Samuel T. (Preacher) Watkins of the Atlanta-Birmingham run, who was to die in 1921 in the wreck of the Kansas City Special near Anniston. He, too, liked the credo, "Trust in the Lord," and had it painted on his cab. He visited jails, taking his brand of rugged railroading religion to shut-ins, and he knelt and prayed before each trip.

Like Daddy Fant, he was a speedster who sometimes frightened his crew as he drove his engine in the hills of Alabama. On one such run his fireman pleaded with him to slow down and he replied easily, "Don't worry. You've got nothing to fear. The Lord's on here with us."

"Maybe he is, Cap'n," said the skeptical fireman, "but He musta got on at Anniston because He sho ain't had time since!"

Most of the doleful old railroad ballads which made the night mawkishly delicious for those gathered around the phonographs in country parlors in some way touched on the lives of Atlanta citizens. These include such tearjerkers as "Ben Dewberry's Final Run," "Wreck of the Royal Palm Express" and, of course, the classic "Wreck of the Old 97."

This song, written by David Graves George of Gretna, Virginia, relates the sad saga of a fast mail express which operated through Atlanta between New York and New Orleans, southbound only. Daddy Fant took the 97 out of Atlanta, but, as music lovers will remember, it was Engineer Joseph A. (Steve) Broady who was bringing her south the day of the wreck.

The song has it:

> They gave him his orders at Monroe, Virginia,
> Saying, "Steve, we're 'way behind time,
> This is not 38 but it's old 97;
> We must put her in Atlanta on time!

And then several quivering stanzas later:

> He was going down grade at ninety miles an hour
> When his whistle broke into a scream.
> He was found in the wreck with his hand on the throttle,
> A-scalded to death by the steam.

To be "on time" was a matter of sacred honor to the old engineer. There was a certain do-you-want-to-live-forever insouciance about their insistence on it. An engineer named Tom Russ, who hauled passenger trains between Atlanta and Macon, had the extra challenge of making up time or, as they put it, "snatching territory" on a short run.

Once when he had time to make up, he is said to have worked his engine with a low reverse roar at her stack "as though her insides were coming out" and left town "with the ten-wheeler snorting like a bull." As he passed under Whitehall Street viaduct, he was "shooting skyrockets out of sight."

A few miles out, a cautious conductor signaled him to slow down. Engineer Russ brought his train to a full stop, got out, walked back to the passanger cars, snatched open a door, found the conductor and addressed him thus: "Listen here, you buggy-rider, if I can stay on that engine up yonder, you certainly can ride the cushions back here! Grab a hold — I'm going to Macon *on time!*"

He did, too, his biographers noted with satisfaction.

During World War II the movement of troops revived the flagging importance of trains. For Atlantans that importance was abundantly underscored. Franklin D. Roosevelt, who may go down in history as the last of the train-riding Presidents, frequently passed through on his way to the Little White House seventy-five miles south of Atlanta at Warm Springs.

Moving a Presidential Special is always a sticky assignment for a railroad, and the Southern's task was magnified by the war. The possibility that an attempt might be made to bomb the President's train was ever present in railroad men's minds. As a precaution the Presidential train was sheathed with armor plate on its bottom side next to the tracks and smaller and heavier doors were installed on the President's car.

So concerned was the railroad with keeping the president alive that it could not foresee the special problem the narrow door would present if he died. While a sorrowing world was still stunned with the news of President Roosevelt's death on April 12, 1945, crews from Atlanta had to be rushed to Warm Springs to deal with a matter of distracting practicality. The door, large enough for a living man, was too small to admit the man in his coffin.

Railroad workers, many of whom knew him personally and loved him, put aside their grief to work far into the night widening the aperture so the President's coffin could be placed aboard without difficulty the next day.

At 10:15 A.M. on Friday, the thirteenth of April 1945, the train moved out from the little flagstop station at Warm Springs. Drawn by two locomotives with bells mournfully clanging, the train that had brought him to his vacation home so many times bore the President back to Washington for the last time. Between Warm Springs and Atlanta crowds of silent, sorrowing people lined up along the railroad tracks to see the train go by.

In Atlanta crowds were of course denser, and at Terminal Station Mayor Hartsfield boarded the train briefly to speak to Mrs. Roosevelt and to present a basket of flowers from the people of Atlanta to their famous part-time neighbor. The next day the *Constitution* ran what had been one of the President's favorite photographs — a picture of him waving jauntily from a train window on one of his early trips through Atlanta. (It was taken by Kenneth Rogers, now retired from the *Constitution* and the Sunday magazine.)

Crimes committed aboard trains keep railroad detectives more than routinely engrossed, but the most sensational crime to involve the railroads is the still-unsolved murder of a handsome opera singer named John Garris on April 21, 1949. Garris, a German-born tenor, who sang here with the Metropolitan Opera Company, was found shot to death in an alley blocks from the railroad yards the morning after the Met had finished its four-day spring engagement here.

Garris had boarded the Met special train shortly before midnight, stowed his luggage away and told fellow singers he was going to play cards for awhile. But the train pulled out without him and Atlanta police and railroad detectives, who flew to Alabama to intercept the train and question members of the Met company, still don't know what happened to entice Garris from the train and to his death.

He was found with a bullet wound near his heart, laid out in a wet, cold alleyway in what police said was "a neat, almost tender way." His coat, unmarked by bullet or by blood, was found on a florist's rubbish heap two blocks away. The valuables and money on his person were undisturbed.

It is a crime railroaders still talk about when night settles down on the yards and the lonesome cry of a long-gone freight moves them to think of life and death and their mysteries.

Oh, you could hear cries of the trains at night wherever you slept in Atlanta. You could feel the pulse of the big engines sometimes in the daytime when you moved about downtown. And it may take you a long time to listen and hear in it again the brawling laughter of the Irish right-of-way builders, the bravado of that pushing, growing frontier town, the bloody battles that were fought over the railroads, the corny ballads, the shrill and biggity noises of commerce. But once you heard it, you knew it for what it was — Atlanta's heartbeat.